Fix Your Supply Chain

*How to Create a Sustainable
Lean Improvement Roadmap*

Fix Your Supply Chain

How to Create a Sustainable Lean Improvement Roadmap

Paul C. Husby and Dan Swartwood

CRC Press
Taylor & Francis Group
Boca Raton   London   New York

CRC Press is an imprint of the
Taylor & Francis Group, an **informa** business

A PRODUCTIVITY PRESS BOOK

Productivity Press
Taylor & Francis Group
270 Madison Avenue
New York, NY 10016

© 2009 by Taylor & Francis Group, LLC
Productivity Press is an imprint of Taylor & Francis Group, an Informa business

No claim to original U.S. Government works
Printed in the United States of America on acid-free paper
10 9 8 7 6 5 4 3 2 1

International Standard Book Number-13: 978-1-56327-381-0 (0)

Library of Congress Cataloging-in-Publication Data

Husby, Paul C.
    Fix your supply chain : how to create a sustainable lean improvement roadmap / Paul C. Husby and Dan Swartwood.
        p. cm.
    Includes bibliographical references and index.
    ISBN 978-1-56327-381-0 (hbk. : alk. paper)
    1. Business logistics. 2. Industrial management. I. Swartwood, Dan. II. Title.

HD38.5.H876 2009
658.7--dc22   2009010697

Visit the Taylor & Francis Web site at
http://www.taylorandfrancis.com

and the Productivity Press Web site at
http://www.productivitypress.com

Contents

Preface

We have had great careers. I worked for 3M for 38 years, Dan worked 25 years for 3M and Imation, and together we collected many great memories and learned many lessons. God has blessed us with terrific families, good health, and the desire to continue contributing to the improvement of businesses. During our careers, we have worked with many great colleagues who have contributed to our development. It is our desire to use what we have been given to contribute to the development of others. Since the early 1980s, Lean has been a passion because it generated terrific business results and developed people. Along the way, we have learned and applied the Theory of Constraints, Six Sigma, and the Supply Chain Operations Reference Model as methodologies for improving supply chains.

The majority of businesses today lack the rigorous implementation of known best practices to improve supply chains. This has both intrigued and frustrated me over the span of my career. Dan and I wrote this book to provide a credible path for business executives to follow to get their supply chains on a path to sustainable excellence.

There are many people who have contributed significantly to this book. First, Dan Swartwood, my coauthor, friend, and coworker in a 3M plant for a dozen years. Dan's contribution to this work is significant, and as I learned 25 years ago when we faced many difficult challenges together, he is a pleasure to work with. All have formative experiences in their lives; most of the time they are the result of extremely difficult challenges that have been faced and overcome.

This was the case with Dan and me. Along with our colleagues at the 3M Weatherford, Oklahoma Data Storage Products Plant, we faced the possibility of having the plant shut down, which would have caused the loss of hundreds of jobs. We were fortunate to have excellent business and manufacturing executives, who challenged us by giving us the liberty, encouragement, and support to take risks in transforming the plant. The team searched for solutions and quickly focused on the continuous improvement practices coming from Japan, learning from some of the early pioneers such as Richard Schoenberger. We were also fortunate during this time to be visited by Masaaki Imai, from whom we received valuable learning and encouragement. He summarized his observations from those visits in his 1986 book, *Kaizen*. The entire plant team pulled together and the business returned to profitability. It continued to operate through the end of the life cycle of diskettes.

The second formative experience was the five years I served as managing director of 3M Brazil. The market was aggressively opening and inward investment increased rapidly, completely changing Brazil's competitive environment. Customers had choices, and in many markets 3M suddenly had strong new competitors. I was blessed with a great team and we worked together to completely transform 3M Brazil from an internally focused company accustomed to a closed market to a market–customer driven company. The organization was realigned, processes were reengineered, and an Enterprise Resource Planning (ERP) system was installed to provide needed information and institutionalize customer-driven processes.

I will always have a strong emotional connection to my colleagues and everyone who was a part of the company during those years. We learned many lessons together, lessons we applied throughout our careers. I will always consider it a blessing to have had so many wonderful people cross my path.

The beautiful woman in my life, Nancy Lillis, was not only very encouraging as I worked on this book, but as a journalism major, she did her best to make a writer out of me.

Paul C. Husby

Launching my career in 1975 with 3M Company was the beginning of an incredible learning experience. There is nothing like the "survival" message to bring focus, and that is exactly what energized our organization to succeed. Twenty percent cost improvement year-on-year was the requirement that necessitated aggressive and continuous improvement. Two of the most important lessons I learned were the following:

1. The opportunity to improve is inexhaustible. The manufacture of diskettes began at a cost of well over $1 each and, near the end of their lives, were being produced (in the United States) at $.07 each. We faced what we thought was an impossible goal numerous times only to learn that it was achievable.

2. There is no substitute for persistence. While faced with a nagging process problem that seemed to defy all solutions, a process engineer shared the results of his latest experiment with me. It had also failed. But he said something I will never forget: "We have found one more unsuccessful solution to this problem. We must be getting very close." It was from people such as this engineer that I learned what continuous improvement really means.

As a management consultant for the past seven years, I have helped companies apply Lean, Six Sigma, and Supply Chain Operations Reference (SCOR) model methodologies to improve competitiveness and operational efficiency. I am a committed believer that these methods are synergistic and hold the key to optimizing continuous improvement in our organizations.

My intention for this book, as is Paul's, is to provide a guide for business executives that will help them accelerate and sustain improvement across their supply chains.

The contributors to this book are many, but I must start with my wonderful wife, who has been my close partner in everything for the past 33 years. Along with our two daughters, we have had many wonderful experiences that have done much to shape my worldview.

The contributor list continues with my longtime friend and mentor, Paul Husby. His contribution is significant to this work and his experience as a change agent and leader at 3M led the way for our success in the data storage business. I have enjoyed this chance to renew our working relationship. Finally, I want to recognize all the great coworkers from 3M, Imation, PRAGMATEK, and Satellite Logistics Group who have walked the improvement path and taught me so much.

Dan Swartwood

Introduction

In their 1994 book *Built to Last* (New York: Harper Business), Jim Collins and Jerry Porras chronicled ten companies that had shown sustainability. Ten years later in 2004, a *Fast Company* article (November 2004), "Was *Built to Last* Built to Last?" by Jennifer Reingold and Ryan Underwood, looked back at how these companies fared over time. They summarized their findings by saying, "In the years since the *Built to Last* book, almost half of the visionary companies on the list have slipped dramatically in performance and reputation, and their vision currently seems more blurred than clairvoyant. Consider the fates of Motorola, Ford, Sony, Walt Disney, Boeing, Nordstrom, and Merck. Each has struggled in recent years, and all have faced serious questions about their leadership and strategy. Odds are, none of them today would meet *Built to Last* criteria for visionary companies, which required that they be the premier player in their industry and be widely admired by people in the know" (p. 2).

While some of these companies have recovered some of their previous greatness, long-term sustained leadership performance has eluded all but a handful of companies. None of us is guaranteed indefinite success in our businesses. The challenge is to create renewal-ensuring sustainable operational excellence. Many factors go into competitive advantage, and it is extremely difficult to identify companies that are truly sustainable now or will be 100 years in the future.

Robert Waterman makes this point very well in his 1987 book *The Renewal Factor* (New York: Bantum), that valid, sustainable market leadership requires constant attention and renewing. The intention of business strategy is to build and sustain competitive advantage as a market leader. In their 1995 book, *Discipline of Market Leaders* (Reading, MA: Addison Wesley), Michael Treacy and Fred Wiersema do an excellent job of connecting business strategy with operational requirements to ensure strategic intentions are carried out by operations driven with clear metrics. They state that market leaders focus on one of three market disciplines as the source of their competitive advantage: (1) operational excellence,

(2) product leadership, and (3) customer intimacy. They also list four rules followed by market leaders:

1. Provide the best marketplace offering by excelling in a specific dimension of value
2. Maintain threshold standards on other dimensions of value
3. Dominate your market by improving year after year
4. Build a well-tuned operating model dedicated to delivering unmatched value

Three of these rules are particularly relevant to our discussion of supply chain performance. The first is Rule 2: *Maintain threshold standards on other dimensions of value.* Maintaining threshold performance means you must have industry parity on all dimensions of competitive performance to avoid being at a disadvantage versus market competitors. The speed of global markets is continuing to raise the bar on minimum threshold levels below which a company is competitively disadvantaged.

The second is Rule 3: *Dominate your market by improving year after year.* Companies must continuously improve capability forever.

Rule 4 is also relevant: *Build a well-tuned operating model dedicated to delivering unmatched value.* This well-tuned operating model must be designed into a company's DNA to ensure delivery of their chosen value discipline. It is critical in defining the performance attributes of the supply chain that must be maintained at the highest levels in the market. This is frequently a major source of failure in companies. We make significant investments in product development and marketing to define product specifications, do customer research, perform market tests, and so forth. Why don't companies put the same rigor into defining the services, costs of goods sold, and working capital requirements? Too many companies are satisfied to set arbitrary metrics and standards of service, costs, and working capital that are not defined to support their "market discipline." Even a strategy based on customer intimacy requires great execution or it will become just a warm fuzzy that doesn't sustain results. Product excellence and differentiation will not sustain a leader's position without good service and competitive value based on a deep understanding of the customer.

The bottom line: *Operational excellence is required to make any winning business strategy sustainable.* Operational excellence is achieved and sustained only through continuous improvement. Sustained continuous improvement requires that a company evaluate current performance against some standard and to implement plans that close identified gaps. It should be intuitively obvious that unless we want this operational excellence achievement to be a one-time event, we must put in place the mechanism to continually evaluate our performance. Companies that fail to improve, at least at the rate of the market movers and shakers, will ultimately lose market position and possibly fail completely. The cold hard fact that operational excellence is a temporary condition at best eludes most companies entirely. The greatest frustration, having led improvement efforts at numerous companies, is seeing well-trained, talented people with enormous opportunity and adequate data achieve only superficial results. What are the barriers?

We tell ourselves a number of comforting things that allow us not to act. You can make up your own list, but some of the most common excuses are the following:

1. *I'm too busy!* It's true everyone is busy just running the day-to-day business. All of our plates are full even beyond what we have time to do. There is no time left to put on our strategic hats and devote the necessary time to continuous improvement.

2. *Change is too painful!* This statement contains some truth. Continuous improvement is painful because it means change, and most people have one thing in common—they avoid pain or change whenever possible. People have a tendency to look at problems such as declining profitability as an event, and once it is fixed, they believe they can go back to business as usual.

3. *Things aren't as bad as they seem!* Humans have an amazing ability to rationalize their situation and explain away performance gaps, especially if the data is sending mixed messages. While sorting out the messages, the organization waits, sometimes misinformed as to the true situation. Perhaps the company has bad competitive intelligence or has rationalized its situation so that it seems as if no action is required. As the saying goes, "Reality is the leading cause of stress." Most people would rather not deal with reality if there is any other alternative.

4. *It's out of our control!* The company is a victim of being in a competitive market; the union, the government, foreign competition, and unfair trade laws are to blame—the responsibility is everyone's

but ours. Since the situation is out of our control, there is nothing to be done. Adopting a victim mentality is fatal.

5. *It's not possible!* History and people's own personal experiences shape their paradigms; therefore, if they have never reduced operational cost by 20 percent in one year, they just can't see how it is possible. If they have never manufactured a product with less than a five-day cycle time, then it's just not believable that four hours is possible. History is full of examples where clear vision and a refusal to fail led to impossible accomplishments.

Also, it can feel as if continuous improvement is being achieved even when it is not. For one thing, it depends on how *improvement* is defined. For some, improvement can be measured as cost avoidance, but the reality is that unless costs are decreasing, working capital returns are increasing, and customer satisfaction is increasing, no improvement exists; it is an illusion.

In this book, we will explore seven factors that can help a company become one of the few that truly achieve and maintain operational excellence.

1. *Top company leadership.* Top company leadership is responsible and accountable for ensuring operational excellence. Vision, accountability, resources, recognition, and energy are the fuel required by the organization from this group; without this, no company will maintain a market leadership position.

2. *Improvement methodology.* There are many prescribed methodological options for continuous improvement, all of which were developed to address specific issues in specific supply chain areas. A baseline understanding of each methodology is important to practitioners, so each methodology needs to be described at a level detailed enough to provide credible working definitions.

3. *Continuous improvement strategy.* Much is published about each methodology, which frequently causes great confusion and misunderstanding. An improvement strategy addresses how we are going to improve. The challenge is to ensure that the methodology selected will address all areas of the supply chain in both assessment and improvement plan implementation.

4. *The cause and the vision.* A cause and a vision are crucial. A company's capacity to embrace change is directly related to its real or

perceived threats. One trait of visionary leaders is their ability to "read the tea leaves," so to speak, and to bring future threats into today's world, preparing the organization for change. Organizations convinced about their global threats believe they have control and the ability to meet the challenges. They feel empowered and committed to making the needed changes. Companies are surrounded by improvement opportunity. It is common when analyzing a value stream map to find less than 5 percent of activities are value-added activities, but it is estimated that only 2 percent of companies implementing Lean achieve any measurable bottom line. Lack of opportunity is not the issue; lack of a cause and a vision *is*. Everyone needs motivation to change, or to put it another way, people will not change *unless* it is more painful to remain where they are.

Motivation within companies can come from numerous sources. Sometimes there is a threat of an imminent shutdown when costs are too high, quality or service is poor, or products no longer appeal to customers. Sometimes the threat is staring everyone in the face and sometimes it feels like a distant cloud that may or may not materialize. Take the auto industry, for example. U.S. automakers have been well aware of the growing threat from Japanese automakers for years. They watched their dominant position gradually erode until Toyota overtook GM as the world's largest automaker. Whatever the reasons—superior quality, fuel efficiency, durability—these gaps have been clear for some time, yet efforts to reverse this trend haven't been successful.

5. *The sustainable improvement roadmap.* Implementation or action must follow planning, training, and strategizing. If the troops don't move to the front line, then the war cannot be won. Lean, Six Sigma, the Theory of Constraints, or the best practice approach of the Supply Chain Operations Reference (SCOR) model are all offered as *must dos* for anyone serious about improvement. Is there a better way to approach your strategy for supply chain operational improvement? Is it necessary to choose one or is there a logical way these approaches can be integrated into a more effective and comprehensive approach to supply chain performance improvement?

6. *Enablement of sustainability.* Enablement speaks to all the other factors, such as culture, IT systems, organizational skills, measurements, rewards, and leadership that support success.

7. *Constancy of purpose.* Constancy of purpose has to live on even when events, such as forecasting time, end of the year, or a new CEO, interfere with the master plan. The urgent cannot be allowed to displace the important. Achieving and maintaining operational excellence is a long-term endeavor, so there must be consistency of purpose across generations of company leadership.

This book brings together the authors' collective 70 years experience in the application of Lean, Six Sigma, SCOR, and the Theory of Constraints. It also brings forward a powerful argument that the current set of improvement systems, methodologies, and tools can be integrated to create a more powerful operational improvement strategy. Is this the answer for all time? Certainly not. Our free markets fuel the creative juices of people around the world, and someday there may be a better operational system than Lean, a better analytical methodology than SCOR, a better approach to quality improvement than Six Sigma, and a better way to approach identifying and removing bottlenecks than the Theory of Constraints, but these are the approaches and tools we have today.

All companies can be more competitive and make step function changes in operational improvement; it is a choice. Once the choice is made, there is a way to achieve this goal through the effective integration and application of the current approaches. It is not better pistols or a silver bullet that is needed; it is cowboys committed to being the best and doing what is necessary to be the best. Lean, Six Sigma, SCOR, and the Theory of Constraints are all widely used and have proven track records in their own rights, but are the improvement approaches competing or complementary? How does anyone make sense out of all these approaches to improving supply chains? What is needed is a model, some clear *how to* instructions, and some examples to understand enough to implement this approach and get results.

WHY YOU NEED THIS BOOK

This book is written by business leaders for business leaders. Improving your business is the goal of improvement methodologies and the focus of this book. Whether you are intimately familiar with the supply chain discipline or have limited experience, this book provides a valuable road-map that can be applied to supply chain improvement. You will gain sufficient understanding of how to lead supply chain improvement to feel confident in taking your company on this important journey.

This Introduction through Chapter 3 offers an understanding of successful supply chain improvement requirements and methodologies, their strengths, and limitations. Chapters 4 and 5 cover the use of these methodologies in a story about Twin City Manufacturing. The company is fictitious, but the experiences and improvement processes are based on the authors' actual experiences. Chapters 6 and 7 are dedicated to enabling and sustaining long-term change. It is beyond the scope of this book to provide detailed training; however, in the resource section we identify many excellent books and training materials you may wish to consult on improvement systems and methodologies.

We have learned many important lessons from our combined 70 years of experience with all supply chain–related functions, in addition to numerous manager and executive assignments. You will find many *Learned from Experience* boxes to reinforce key points with real-life experiences.

LEARNED FROM EXPERIENCE: DAN AND PAUL

THE FEAR OF DEATH CAN BE AN INCREDIBLE MOTIVATOR

In 1980, the Data Recording Products division of 3M produced two main products, rigid disks and diskettes. At the time, rigid disks dominated the business, but after three years, the division was in trouble. This was our wake-up call. It was now clear that our survival business depended on achieving a much higher level of performance. We transitioned from a state of modest motivation to one of intense motivation.

The book is based on our collective experience, which we share both to help others learn and to continue to push our own learning along the continuous improvement journey.

HOW TO USE THIS BOOK

We wrote this guide for a variety of leaders, including

- CEOs
- Corporate and business unit leaders
- Marketing and sales leaders

This resource will help them understand the concepts, principles, tools, and factors critical to success.

If you fall among these leaders, to get the most from this book, we recommend that you concentrate on the following:

1. Chapter 1 to understand the requirements for continuous improvement
2. Chapter 2 to learn about the most common improvement methodologies
3. Chapter 3 for a comparative analysis of improvement methodologies
4. Chapter 4, pages 67–77, for how to build a continuous improvement process
5. Chapter 5, pages 107–118, for how to implement a continuous improvement process
6. Chapter 6 to gain an understanding of the enabling requirements vital to sustaining continuous improvement and
7. Chapter 7 to learn why constancy of purpose is essential for building a decade or decades of continuous improvement

If you are a manufacturing leader, we suggest that you read the entire book including the details covered in Chapters 4 and 5 as Twin City Manufacturing goes through a transformation. The principles, concepts, and tools come to life through charts, data, and dialogue as you follow the company as it implements its transformation.

1

The Seven Components of Sustainable Supply Chain Improvement

The Supply Chain Council (SCC) defines a *supply chain* as "the integrated processes of Plan, Source, Make, Deliver, and Return spanning from the suppliers' supplier to the customers' customer." The key word in this definition is *integrated*. A supply chain is not defined by only the product or the customer; it needs to consider both to ensure integration of the external customer's view with the internal product view. The supply chain of a company controls many aspects of the customer's experience and is the critical execution component of a company's strategy. If your products are better than your competitors' but your service is worse, an innovative product strategy is not likely to produce the expected results.

The supply chain spans the entire scope of a company's operations, and therefore every function in the company affects it. Marketing may run promotions, set merchandising plans, or create special products or packages for customers, all of which have an impact on the company's supply chain. Product development designs new products, specifies raw materials, and determines product specifications, decisions that have a direct impact on the supply chain. Optimization of supply chain performance requires seamless integration of the core process: Plan, Source, Make, Deliver, and Return. The metrics throughout your company's organization must also be aligned to deliver customer value. Supply chain is a *team sport,* and the CEO is the only position that spans the company's supply chain. The bottom line is: Supply chain execution determines the operational competitive advantage or disadvantage of a company.

As introduced earlier, there are seven components necessary for sustainable supply chain improvement.

TOP LEADERSHIP CHAMPION

Yes, we know, every improvement program says top leadership must champion the process. There is a very simple, logical, and valid reason for this. Producing significant supply chain improvement is a team sport because no other operational process in the company is impacted by every other operational group in the business. Obviously manufacturing, business planning, logistics, and sourcing all have to be on the same page. So do the goals and reward systems of marketing, laboratory development, sales, and finance. All these functions influence the supply chain; therefore, they all must be aligned through strategies, goals, and metrics. For example, if the marketing department continually runs push/load promotions to hit the quarterly numbers, they may get free coffee and donuts when the numbers come in, but do they really understand the total cost of running businesses this way? It is doubtful they do because if they did, they would find alternative ways to accomplish the same goals.

The laboratory specifies a material that is "unique"; it is sourced from Kazakhstan, it has a 90-day lead time and requires a four-month fixed forecast. This decision creates a flexibility constraint, inventory cost, and quality and service risks. The Sales Department needs to make its quarterly quota, so they sell product that is constrained by capacity, then scream and complain about the unresponsiveness of the supply chain organization. Because it wasn't their fault that product couldn't be produced, they are forgiven and given credit for making the quota.

Finance has the allocation formulas and a full costing approach, so no one is interested in making the product line less complex or reducing the number of small customers because those very low-volume products have "nicely reported gross margins."

Haven't these things driven every supply chain professional crazy at one time or another? The supply chain is affected not only by every function in the company, but by organizations outside the company as well. Furthermore, the supply chain doesn't extend only from our customers to purchasing, but also to suppliers' suppliers and customers' customers. As RACI (Responsible, Accountable, Consulted, and Informed) analysis quickly reveals, only the top executives have the "reach" to influence, manage, and remove barriers at the supply chain level. Without top executive champions who are actively engaged, the probability of achieving significant improvement is very low.

LEARNED FROM EXPERIENCE: PAUL

ONLY THE CEO CAN LEAD THE BUILDING OF A CUSTOMER VALUE–DRIVEN OPERATIONAL MODEL

I was the managing director of 3M Brazil from 1995 to 2000. Together with the leadership team, we transformed the company to a true market segment and customer-driven company. After three years, we had made great strides and completely changed the mind-set and processes from selling products to meeting customer needs in the selected segments with complete solutions. The supply chain was also transformed as processes were rebuilt to align completely with our commitment to providing better customer treatment in each segment.

In the fourth year, we implemented an enterprise resource planning (ERP) system to better enable and institutionalize the new processes. Although the supply chain director was one of the best leaders I have worked with, this would have been impossible if it had been just a "supply chain initiative." Step-function supply chain improvement requires that the managing director—the only person who really has end-to-end leadership—be the personal champion.

CONTINUOUS IMPROVEMENT STRATEGY AND METHODOLOGIES

Toyota, GE, Motorola, Allied Signal, and 3M have demonstrated the value of having a companywide continuous improvement strategy led from the top. One can argue about the sustainability of some of these efforts, but that does not detract from the lessons learned. In fact, only Toyota has proven sustainability of continuous improvement. All of these strategies have the following in common:

- The continuous improvement approach was mandated companywide.
- It was led by the top company executive.
- Continuous improvement expectations were integrated into the operating plans and objectives of every unit in the organization.
- The results prove that every organization has great potential to improve significantly.

The conclusion from examining these continuous improvement approaches is clear: Every company must have a companywide continuous improvement strategy and methodology.

Methodologies

To achieve continuous improvement, companies apply four major methodologies. Each of these methodologies has proven value based on the experience and results of companies that applied them successfully. Each of these methodologies was developed as a practical solution to issues faced by the companies who were responsible for their development.

Supply Chain Operations Reference

In the 1990s, PRTM (a management consulting firm with a long history in supply chain) and AMR (a research firm focused on business process and enterprise information technology) introduced the Supply Chain Operations Reference model (SCOR), a top-down supply chain assessment methodology. In 1996, PRTM and AMR founded a user-based organization, the Supply Chain Council. It started with 69 member companies and now has more than 700. SCOR defines a supply chain as "the integrated processes of Plan, Source, Make, Deliver, and Return spanning from the suppliers' supplier to the customers' customer." (See http://www. supplychain.org for the most recent version of the "Supply Chain Operations Reference model.")

SCOR documents current processes using three levels of process decomposition to create an "as is" (present or current) state (see Figure 1.1). Only three levels of SCOR have specific processes defined within the model. Level 4 can be used by the user to define their unique configuration of process details.

Based on the business strategy, a "to be" (future) state supply chain is defined. With a company's basis of competition defined, the second level

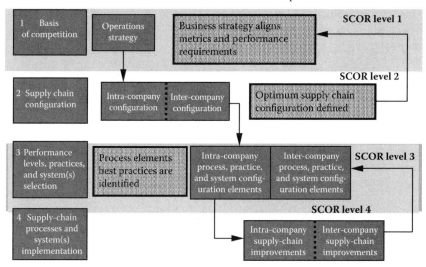

FIGURE 1.1
SCOR improvement process.

of supply chain configuration is completed. The configuration ensures meaningful performance, and best practice comparisons are made as level three is constructed. Benchmarking performance and practices information can be obtained from sources recommended by the Supply Chain Council (many are available at no cost to their members).

The value of quantified gaps in service, cost, and inventory between the two states provides a high-level business case that specifies the value to be gained from achieving the "to be" state. The "to be" state processes and practices are then prioritized into an implementation plan to achieve the performance targeted through the benchmark processes.

Lean Supply Chain System

Lean is a supply chain operational system based on the Toyota Production System, which Toyota has been perfecting for more than five decades. In 1989, James Womack and Daniel Jones popularized the system outside of Japan in their book *The Machine That Changed the World*. The Lean Supply Chain System (Lean) integrates all the participants in the supply chain—supplier, manufacturer, and customer—into one value stream, increasing value to the customer. Lean offers an array of tools that improve the supply chain while building and sustaining the Lean Supply Chain System. In their book *Lean Thinking* (1989), Womack and Jones identify the five key concepts of Lean:

- *Value* is defined by the customer.
- *Value stream* is the information and material flow from suppliers' suppliers to customers' customers.
- *Flow* is the synchronized continuous movement of material through the value stream.
- *Pull* is a product usage signal from the customer to other participants in the supply chain.
- *Perfection* is the never-ending pursuit of zero waste.

Lean applies a unique process mapping approach called Value Stream Mapping. The current-state Value Stream Map documents the materials and information flow. Value stream mapping always starts with the customer and includes both material and information flow. In addition, key information is gathered about each value stream operation.

The second step is the creation of a future-state Value Stream Map, which is done by assuming that lean practices have been applied to the value stream. Projects are identified based on the changes needed to transform current-state processes into future-state processes. Lean tools are then applied to the improvement projects. When projects are completed, the process is repeated to create a new set of projects. This iterative process continues forever in pursuit of perfection.

Six Sigma

Six Sigma can be applied to any process that needs improvement. Potential projects are defined to fill gaps between current performance and the level required to achieve the success of the annual business plan. By targeting the areas of the business plan with the greatest critical gaps, organizational effort is focused and prioritized. Brainstorming and analysis of current processes are then often used for bottom–up generation of potential projects. Process performance may be compared to an *entitlement level*, a level of performance that may represent the best short-term performance ever achieved. It stimulates consideration of the process from a new perspective. Once the projects are defined, the five-step Six Sigma DMAIC (define, measure, analyze, improve, control) process is used.

DMAIC is the primary Six Sigma tool for reducing variability in existing processes. DMAIC, without doubt, has proven itself a very powerful tool for improvement at 3M and a number of other well-known companies. It is a rigorous process that relies heavily on statistical methodologies and techniques. Projects, which follow a prescribed five-step process, are completed within a specified time frame resulting in quick impact on the business. In general, projects are completed in four to six months during the early stages of Six Sigma implementation. When Master Black Belts and Black Belts gain experience they become more proficient. and the length of time required to complete projects decreases.

Black Belts are intensively trained in all Six Sigma DMAIC skills and tools, they are expected to complete projects and coach Green Belts who are leading their own projects (See http://www.sme.org for Six Sigma certification requirements). A Master Black Belt has the same technical skills as a Black Belt but normally is also trained in leadership and program management. They are usually responsible for a number of Black Belts. Most leading Six Sigma practicing companies have their own certification process, which requires successful completion of projects.

Projects are identified by examining the defects affecting the achievement of business objectives or obvious variability in processes. Next, the five-step DMAIC process is applied to resolve the defect. Measurements for projects normally focus on the operation or step in the process that is being improved. Frequently countermeasure metrics are also applied to ensure that the improvement doesn't cause a defect in another area of the process.

Six Sigma requires an investment in infrastructure; that is, the training of Master Black Belts and Black Belts. Because these are normally rotating assignments, a core-training infrastructure is also important to sustained success.

Six Sigma is a great set of tools for reducing defects and variability. It is also valuable in developing leadership and changing company culture to be more data driven. Results achieved at 3M and many other companies speak for themselves—Six Sigma works.

Theory of Constraints

The Theory of Constraints (TOC) was developed by Eli Goldratt and his collaborators. It became broadly known in his 1984 book *The Goal*. TOC views organizations as systems with resources linked together to meet an organization's goal. All systems have a constraint that limits the system's capacity to improve and better meet or exceed its goal. Organizations have limited resources, so it is critical that resources be applied to reduce or eliminate constraints to maximize success.

TOC methodology includes improvement tools. The tools use rigorous root-cause analysis to define the solution. The methodology also identifies all the assumptions and conditions needed to ensure success of a proposed solution. These conditions and assumptions provide action items for implementation plans. TOC improvement tools work equally well for continuous improvement or breakthrough problem solving.

A CAUSE AND A VISION

An organization needs a great reserve of energy to make significant change—change that is sustainable over an extended period. Sustaining this high level of energy and commitment requires constancy of purpose by top leadership who must continually reinforce the need for change and the benefits of success.

The Cause

The first prerequisite of significant change is motivation; people must have a cause that justifies their commitment, energy, creativity, and willingness to change behaviors and practices. Both authors have had experience with businesses that failed or were threatened with failure. As stated in the introduction, the fear of death can be an incredible motivating force. Most companies are not under immediate threat of going out of business, so how do they create the cause that inspires total organizational commitment and energy to make significant change?

The key to creating a cause is in radically changing the lens through which organizations see themselves. There is great strength in changing magnification power to view a wider range of possibilities, a new scale of comparison. The entire competitive field must be viewed while considering long-term threats and sustainability. In short, the organization's perspective about itself and its current levels of performance must change. Chapter 4 will introduce leadership thinking and tools which can be used to create a cause that organizations can relate to and internalize providing a foundation for change.

The Vision

Developing a meaningful vision for the supply chain means developing a new perspective:

- How do you stack up versus the best supply chain practices?
- How do you stack up versus the best supply chain performance?

The vision must state clearly the compelling business case for change. What will be gained? How will the business be different? What will the customer experience?

LEARNED FROM EXPERIENCE: DAN

THE WILL OF AN ORGANIZATION TO CHANGE DEPENDS ON THE WILL OF THE LEADER TO CHANGE

When we were struggling for survival in the 3M diskette business, we encountered this phenomenon. One of our key suppliers was an internal division that was not competitive in cost *or* quality. The corporation required us to source the material internally despite these issues because "It was best for the company!" Our repeated attempts to engage this division in more aggressive improvement efforts were largely ignored. When the leadership of our internal division could not be persuaded to change, we moved to an outside supplier, enduring criticism from many inside the company. It was our obligation as leaders. It was not enough; the division was closed a year later.

SCOR provides key insights into the state of current supply chain performance and practices. It also provides the basis for creating a relevant supply chain vision, one that can be valuable through a three- to five-year journey to sustainable supply chain competitive advantage.

In addition to SCOR, benchmarking, entitlement thinking from Six Sigma, and perfection thinking from Lean create a powerful vision that is connected directly to performance improvement opportunities, which increase customer value.

VALUE CREATION FOR CUSTOMERS THROUGH IMPROVING SUPPLY CHAIN PERFORMANCE

In his 1980 book *Competitive Strategy*, Michael Porter describes strategy as "taking offensive or defensive actions to create a defendable position in an industry, to cope successfully with the five competitive forces and thereby yield a superior return on investment for the firm" (p. 34). He goes on to say, "There are three internally consistent generic strategic approaches to outperforming other firms in an industry: 1) overall cost leadership 2) differentiation 3) focus" (p. 34).

In their 1995 book, *The Discipline of Market Leaders*, Michael Treacy and Fred Wiersema refine this same basic thought as they describe the three value disciplines: (1) operational excellence, (2) product leadership, and (3) customer intimacy. They also introduce four rules that all market leaders must follow regardless of which value discipline they choose as the basic strategy of the business:

- Provide the best marketplace offering by excelling in a specific value dimension.
- Maintain threshold standards on other dimensions of value.
- Dominate your market by improving year after year.
- Build a well-tuned operating model dedicated to delivering unmatched value.

The last three rules are critically dependent on a company's supply chain. Unfortunately, poorly defined metrics are common. How can value be added for customers through supply chain performance if it isn't driven by well-defined metrics? Metrics must define the service attributes that reflect customer value, ultimately leading to a high level of customer satisfaction.

In basic terms, customers have needs that only the supply chain can satisfy. Well-aligned metrics are fundamental to an effective business strategy. Treacy and Wiersema go on to say,

> "In a competitive marketplace, improving customer value is the market leader's imperative. The operating model is the key to raising and resetting customer expectations. Improving it can make competitors' offerings look less appealing, or even shatter their position by rendering their value

proposition obsolete. *The operating model is the market leader's ultimate weapon in the quest for market dominance"* (p. 25).

Customer value is created through supplier contributions to increasing customer profits, sales, and cash. Customer value supply chain potential comes from three areas:

1. *Service*, which includes delivery, product, information, and post sales service
2. *Cost*, which is a customer's cost of doing business with supplying companies
3. *Fixed and working capital*, which is required to maintain inventory

Unfortunately, many companies' supply chain metrics and objectives are not directly driven by customer values. The process for aligning supply chain metrics starts with understanding a customer's cost of doing business with your company. In Chapter 4, we will discuss how to get a clear understanding of the supply chain metrics that drive your customer's EVA (Economic Value Added) analysis. This collaborative process helps clarify your customers' priorities and the joint opportunities that may exist to improve their EVA.

IMPLEMENTATION

With an improvement strategy and methodology in place, a vision set, and customer value improvement understood, it is time for implementation. This is the hard work of leadership: holding the organization accountable, challenging the organization to pursue perfection, coaching, and providing needed resources to achieve the goal. Implementation of transformational change to supply chains requires a three- to five-year time horizon. Changes in practices must be implemented and institutionalized. Leadership needs enough supply chain understanding to know when midcourse corrections are needed. This includes changing team members when it is clear they are not capable or don't have the will to be successful. Improvement progress should be integrated into every operational review with business unit leaders being expected to report on progress.

ENABLEMENT

Enablement refers to aspects of the company that support change, particularly culture, metrics, rewards, skills, organizational structure, information technology (IT) systems, and leadership development. Enablement is often the source of failure and commonly overlooked, so it must be built into implementation plans from the beginning.

Culture

Organizational culture can make or break any improvement effort. Certain aspects of a culture resist change, while other aspects or best practices help an organization embrace change. For example, does the organizational culture encourage or discourage involvement at all levels? If production employees are rarely asked for input and there is no sharing of business issues and performance, how can they be expected to feel and act like stakeholders?

Organizations develop a cultural lens through which they view the outside world. The culture of an organization is important to getting work done and giving team members a feeling of stability. The cultural lens frequently makes it difficult for organizations to embrace significant change, change which challenges the way things are done. Successful implementation of significant supply chain change requires understanding the organization's culture. Company leadership effort is needed to convince the organization to secure the future and fully embrace needed change.

Metrics and Rewards

Lack of metric alignment with rewards is frequently an obstacle in supply chain performance. Sustainable supply chain competitive advantage is not achievable in organizations with conflicting metrics among the various functions. If manufacturing is measured mostly on cost, those involved are likely to make it a higher priority than service and inventory in an effort to meet their objectives. If sales is only measured by top line sales, they are likely to sell those products that are easier to sell regardless of the profit margin or capacity available. Company leadership must ensure that metrics and rewards systems of all the company's functions are tightly aligned in support of supply chain performance improvement. Applying the SCOR methodology facilitates alignment and prioritization of metrics across your organization, increasing the probability of supply chain improvement success.

Skills

Organizational knowledge and skills are evident through examination of a company's practices and business processes. Most organizations have individuals with extensive knowledge and skills at the top; but vast untapped resources in most companies are shop floor operational team members who are less trained and uninvolved. If employees were not provided training that supports improvement, such as analytical problem solving or teamwork, why would they exhibit these behaviors?

The U.S. military is a good example. Every soldier is eventually trained in a specialty, but not until each has completed basic training. Basic training ensures that everyone has essential skills that maximize the unit's probability of achieving its mission. Why doesn't this analogy apply to all businesses? We all have a mission to satisfy/delight our customers, our shareholders, and ourselves.

SCOR methodology provides an excellent assessment approach to understanding an organization's knowledge. A company's current practice level is an accurate reflection of the organization's knowledge. It is not in the scope of this book to address the specific knowledge required to implement the best practices that lead to supply chain excellence. It *is* in our scope to provide the references and resources for readers to gain specific Six Sigma, Lean, and SCOR knowledge. (See Resources, page 181.)

Organization Structure

A company's organizational structure is established and modified for a variety of reasons, such as increasing focus, realigning resources, increasing end-to-end accountability, leveraging specific leadership skills, decentralizing decision making, centralizing decision making, and aligning with changes in strategic direction. Over time, a company may appear to make organizational changes that reverse previous changes as it adapts to changing business environments and competitive challenges. Organizational structure is a key leadership tool that needs to be employed to best use the company's talent in pursuit of its goals.

IT Systems

Effective information systems are fundamental to institutionalizing the processes, practices, data, and metrics that support continuous improvement. Our systems, data-gathering processes, and particularly data reporting must support customer value and the improvement of operational processes. This usually means simplifying what we are doing in the operational processes, reducing complexity, and eliminating excessive data collection and ineffective controls.

Before IT systems can be effectively implemented, the Lean data model processes and practices must be well established. There is a temptation to move quickly to IT systems to "help" implement the Lean System. Consider this carefully. What appears to be inefficiency in using manual approaches often facilitates easy changes that improve processes.

In addition, running manual operational systems often facilitates operational team members' understanding of the systems. Most people don't understand the process being performed by the computer. They view it as a black box. We need all operational team members engaged in continuous improvement. This requires simple, visual, transparent systems that allow everyone to be a full team member.

The Lean operating system is built on the premise that only the direct production operations team member adds value to the customer, so IT systems must be designed and implemented in support of the frontline operators. IT systems are important to effective supply chain management, but they must be designed and applied to *enable* the operational processes, not define them.

Leadership Development

It is very unlikely that a company will create long-term value over time without having excellent leadership. Many companies such as GE are widely recognized for leadership development using a formal development process. Every company that desires to create long-term sustainable market value must have a dedicated process for leadership development that provides strong strategic and operational skills and capability.

CONSTANCY OF PURPOSE

It is truly amazing to think Toyota has practiced Lean for more than 50 years. The Toyota Production System is part of the company's DNA. The challenge of implementing sustainable supply chain improvement in a company cannot be overstated. Transformational supply chain operational change requires changing the way management thinks and what management does. It takes years to achieve a mature state, and as the baton of management leadership passes from one generation to another, commitment to sustainable supply chain improvement must be constant or people will return to the old ways of doing things. Continuously repeating assessment and improvement cycles over decades is the proof of constancy of purpose.

In summary, the seven components of sustainable supply chain improvement are about leaders taking ownership of their company's supply chain, not delegating this important source of competitive advantage to company supply chain professionals.

REFERENCES

Goldratt, Eli, and Jeff Cox. *The goal*. Great Barrington, MA: North River Press, 1984.

Porter, Michael. *Competitive strategy*. New York: Free Press, 1980.

Treacy, Michael, and Fred Wiersema. *The discipline of market leaders*. Reading, MA: Addison Wesley, 1995.

Womack, James, and Daniel Jones. *Lean thinking*. New York: Free Press, 2000.

Womack, James P., Daniel T. Jones, and Daniel Roos. *The machine that changed the world*. New York: Rawson Associates, 1989.

2

Improvement Methodologies
Six Sigma, Lean, Theory of
Constraints, and SCOR

Unquestionably, the decades since World War II have brought ever-accelerating change in the global competitive environment, driven by the rapid increase in global market access. Competitive markets have also stimulated significant change in supply chain thinking and practices. The history of supply chain improvement through better ideas and technology can be tracked nearly 200 years (see Figure 2.1). A review through the lens of the last 60 years of supply chain practices and systems helps to understand the origins and evolution of current dominant supply chain practices as well as improvement methodologies.

Taiichi Ohno began developing the Toyota Production System (TPS) in 1953. He and his colleagues worked tirelessly for 20 years to fully develop and deploy the TPS processes and practices across the company and their key suppliers. The major contribution of TPS, or what we now call the Lean system, is improved value for customers forever through flow, pull, elimination of all forms of waste, and the pursuit of perfection.

The introduction of Material Requirements Planning (MRP) in the 1970s brought tremendous advances in forecasting, planning, and scheduling. Planning became time-phased, rendering reorder point methods obsolete for inventory management of dependent demand items in manufacturing operations. The concepts of forecast-based and time-phased planning works well in a stable demand-and-supply plan environment, but this "perfect plan assumption" exists only in textbooks. We all recognize the futility of trying to create perfectly stable and level demand plans. The

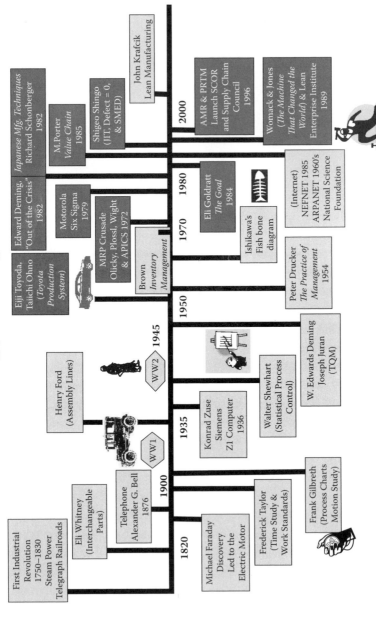

Supply Chain Chronology

FIGURE 2.1
Supply chain chronology.

other big contribution of MRP is the use of forecasts to drive the reorder point inventory control method for independent demand items, such as finished goods.

Since the introduction of MRP, we have learned about the infamous *bullwhip effect* on inventory and demand stability. What starts as level demand at the end user is amplified as it passes upstream through distributor, manufacturer, and raw material supplier, becoming highly variable because of economic lot sizing, which occurs at each supply chain level. The Lean best practice of creating a pull signal based on actual consumption for independent demand items resolves this issue without creating new ones. This practice has been known in the United States since 1982, yet a majority of companies still operate with the *perfect plan assumption* and the resulting push planning model.

The next key contribution to supply chain practices came in the late 1970s, when Motorola introduced the Six Sigma quality improvement methodology. The rigorous statistical analysis tools of Six Sigma have been used in manufacturing by process and quality engineers since Walter Shewhart introduced statistical process control in the 1930s. Motorola created Six Sigma to institutionalize the use of these statistical tools and implement them through a top-down companywide deployment focused on improving product quality. There are many well-documented Six Sigma successes from companies such as GE, Allied Signal, and 3M. They built on the initial success of Motorola to create a more robust set of tools, applying them across all company operations, further validating the value of Six Sigma.

In the early 1980s, consulting companies introduced the concepts and terminology of supply chain and quality improvement gurus such as Edward Deming, who recognized that successful companies need to make improvement in the context of their entire supply chain network. During this time, North America learned about Toyota's use of JIT (just-in-time) manufacturing and kanban from Richard Schonberger's book *Japanese Manufacturing Techniques* (1982).

Lean manufacturing gained implementation traction in 1989 with the publication of James Womack and Daniel Jones's book *The Machine That Changed the World* (1989). Shigeo Shingo made numerous contributions to Lean through his teaching, consulting, and books about Lean. Eli Goldratt introduced the Theory of Constraints (TOC) in his 1984 book *The Goal*. Its system view of operations and the understanding that all systems have constraints has more than 20 years of well-documented contributions to its credit.

The final key contribution to supply chain continuous improvement was the 1996 launch by AMR & PRTM of SCOR (the Supply Chain Operations Reference model) and the Supply Chain Council's end-to-end supply chain assessment methodology. This was a significant milestone in creating a user-controlled common language and methodology. The participation of 700 companies and the growing global presence of the Supply Chain Council is evidence of the continuing value SCOR is generating for user companies.

Given this success, why hasn't a common language and methodology for supply chain assessment and improvement been adopted across all manufacturing and service companies?

This chronology of significant contributions to supply chain practices and continuous improvement clearly demonstrates that each of these events occurred as contributors built on previous contributors' knowledge and practice gaps. Each of the contributors solved a previously unsolved problem or improved on a previous contribution, taking it to a deeper systemic level than the original practice had. Recognizing the evolutionary nature of supply chain theory and practice reinforces the argument of this book that thinking and most of the common practices for designing and operating supply chains are synergistic. To begin to understand this synergism, we must first establish operational definitions of the four most commonly applied improvement methodologies.

OPERATIONAL DEFINITIONS

An in-depth examination of operational definitions, strengths, and limitations of Six Sigma, Lean, the Theory of Constraints, and SCOR will help identify the complementary and conflicting elements of each, and understand how they function independently. It will also provide the foundation for later chapters where we discuss the convergence of these approaches to create a sustainable competitive advantage using a Sustainable Improvement Roadmap (SIR). (See the Resources Section for a list of materials and organizations that provide training and information that will help implement these four methodologies.)

Six Sigma

Six Sigma has a defined set of process improvement steps, known as DMAIC (define, measure, analyze, improve, control). In addition, it has tools for designing products to ensure customer satisfaction and reliability called the Design for Six Sigma. Only the DMAIC methodology, which is the Six Sigma tool used to improve existing processes, will be dealt with in this discussion. The purpose of DMAIC is to improve growth, cost, or working capital performance of a business. It is a five-step improvement methodology based on the vigorous use of statistical methods (Figure 2.2 illustrates the various tools included in the five steps). Potential improvement projects receive high priority when their elimination or improvement is necessary to achieve the annual business plan; for example, defects that result in customer dissatisfaction, high cost, high inventories, or other negative financial measures. Once the "hopper" of potential projects is identified, the projects are prioritized to align with the business's priorities and started through the five-step process.

The Six Sigma process model is shown in Figure 2.3. The process turns input X's into output Y. This terminology is important, so take a moment look at the model if you are not familiar with Six Sigma.

> **Six Sigma** DMAIC is a methodology for reducing variation, decreasing defects, and improving quality when the root cause is unknown and not easily identifiable.

Define	Measure	Analyze	Improve	Control
Project charter	Process map	Multi-vari study	Pilot study	Control plan summary
Process definition	C & E matrix	Hypothesis testing	Designed Experiment	Dashboard
Business metric being improved	FMEA	Statistical tests	If the solution is obvious, implement it	Process documentation
Process defect	Collect data			Acceptance strategies
Project Y= key process output	Apply appropriate statistical tools			Audit plan
Project Y entitlement	Measurement Systems Analysis			
Project metrics	Capability study			
Business impact				
Scope and boundaries				

FIGURE 2.2
Six Sigma DMAIC.

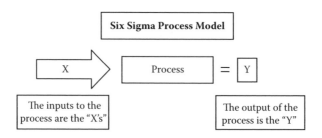

FIGURE 2.3
Six Sigma process model.

Six Sigma DMAIC identifies defects (Y's) in the output of processes that need improvement through better control of key input and process variables (X's).

The basics of the five steps are as follows:

Define: What is the undesirable process variability or defect that must be eliminated? This is the most critical of the five steps and the most common source of project failures. Without proper scoping, projects are formulated that try to "solve the world's problems" and, as a result, are never finished or the team is distracted as it chases spurious issues unrelated to the project. Proper project scoping keeps the team focused on getting improvements implemented. In this step, the process that is to be improved is studied and specific defects that need to be eliminated or parameters that need to be improved are defined. A Six Sigma practice used to stimulate creativity by setting aggressive goals is called *entitlement thinking*. Project participants look for positive performance outliers and ask, "Why can't the process perform like this every day?"

The define step provides a clear project goal, such as: What is the benefit if there is zero waste and a well-defined project charter which

1. is driven by a business strategy and a business plan improvement goal,
2. reflects the voice of the customer in project metrics,
3. clearly defines project objectives, and
4. defines the scope of the project appropriately to ensure it can be accomplished in four to six months or less.

Measure: What is the measurement of the project (Y)? A project's measurement phase defines the current process, establishes metrics, and validates the measurement quality. It should document the current process, identify inputs and outputs, establish process capability of the critical parameter (Y) selected for improvement, determine current measurement system capability, and develop a cause-and-effect matrix to identify critical input variables(s).

Analyze: What are the root causes of variation? Here the potential sources of process variability are identified by

1. selecting enough input variables (X's) to make analysis feasible,
2. using multivari studies to determine which X's have the most impact on the project (Y), and
3. planning initial improvement activities.

Improve: What improvements will eliminate the root causes? Relationships between critical X's and the project (Y) are quantified and selected to verify the proposed solutions by

1. determining the effect critical X's have on the project (Y) using designed experiments,
2. developing the sequence of experiments,
3. identifying the critical inputs that need to be controlled,
4. defining and piloting solutions to resolve problem root causes.

Control: What controls will ensure that the improvement arrived at is institutionalized and that the root cause of the problem is permanently resolved? The project control phase ensures that the process maintains the gains achieved, is neutral or positive for customers, and controls the critical X's through

1. a well-executed control plan,
2. the identification of the control plan process owner, and
3. tracking financial results for a year.

SIX SIGMA INFRASTRUCTURE REQUIREMENTS

Six Sigma success requires a significant investment in infrastructure. A program office must be established with a high-level leader responsible for implementation, training, and coaching. Credible outside training support is necessary, even if the organization has qualified people with the knowledge and skills to support the statistical analysis. Training of Black Belts can take four weeks and projects are likely to average six months during the initial twelve to eighteen months of a Six Sigma Program. Therefore, it may take as much as a year to become proficient in Six Sigma tool application and completely self-sufficient in Six Sigma. Each business unit and/or function must establish a hierarchy of Master Black Belts (MBB) and Black Belts (BB). MBBs and BBs must be the best talent in the organization and must hold two-year full time assignments to develop their Six Sigma and leadership competencies. Eventually all salaried personnel must be trained at least as Green Belts (GB); in addition, leaders must be trained to effectively champion the cause. Once trained, everyone is expected to be a contributing member to projects.

Figure 2.4 provides an operational definition of Six Sigma, but Six Sigma goes far beyond solving problems; it significantly improves leadership development because

1. MBB and BB assignments require leadership to mobilize project teams and get results, although the positions have no real direct organizational authority;
2. cross-functional projects give MBBs and BBs the opportunity to learn about other functions in the organization; and
3. a collaborative global network of MBBs and BBs shares the experience for two years; these relationships will certainly be productive for many years after their Six Sigma experience.

Six Sigma DMAIC Operational Definitions

Definition	A structured improvement methodology using a standard approach and statistical tools
Purpose	• Reduce process variability • Eliminate defects
Project Identification	Keys issues or process problems
Problem Solving	Prescriptive DMAIC problem-solving method
Performance Measurement	Specific process and project metrics
Infrastructure/ Engagement	• Six Sigma expertise • MBB/BB/GB resources • Ad hoc teams

FIGURE 2.4
Six Sigma operation definition.

Six Sigma also changes an organization's culture by

1. creating a common language, tool set, and methodology for people companywide to solve problems and improve business;
2. building collaboration across businesses and functions, cross-functional projects, and teams; and
3. normalizing better data-based decision making.

LEAN SYSTEM

In his book, *Toyota Production System* (TPS, translated and made available in English through Productivity Press, 1988), Taiichi Ohno (Toyota engineer and manager, and later president of Toyota Motor Company) tells his story of beginning and developing the Toyota Production System. Toyoda Kiichiro, the founder of Toyota Motor Company, was challenged by his father Toyoda Sakichi to start an automobile manufacturing company. When World War II ended, Toyoda Kiichiro discovered American automobile manufacturers were nine times more productive than Toyota. He, in turn, challenged Taiichi Ohno to catch up with America in three years.

These three leaders recognized that to become competitive would require the elimination of waste. This stimulated their radical thinking, which led to the values and principles that formed the conceptual basis for TPS. Toyota is not only the world's largest car company, but also produces more profit than all other carmakers combined. The Toyota production system (Lean) is now part of Toyota's DNA, but it has taken decades to perfect it.

The more one understands about Lean, the more one marvels at Ohno's TPS. It is difficult to understand how they know "the footsteps of every operator every day," yet the employee relations environment has been positive enough for Toyota plants to remain union free in the United States. This is one of the many counterintuitive lessons to be learned from a serious study of the Lean system. How do they continue to improve after 50 years of using the same system?

Ohno's book also illuminates the people and experiences that influenced his thinking and the values leading to Lean, an operating system that transforms the entire supply chain. In the book he wrote, "A total management system is needed that develops human ability to its fullest capacity and fruitfulness, utilizes facilities and machines well, and eliminates all waste. This system will work for any type of business" (p. 9). The Lean Supply Chain System (see Figure 2.5) is predicated on four clear values and seven principles, and has as its goal eliminating waste and increasing customer value forever by optimizing people, materials, space, and equipment resources. It specifies seven forms of waste to be eliminated:

1. Overproduction—making more than is needed
2. Transport—excessive movement of materials
3. Motion—inefficient movement of people
4. Waiting—underutilization of people
5. Inventory—material lying around unused
6. Overprocessing—manufacturing to a higher quality standard than expected by the customer
7. Defect correction—time spent fixing defects, including the part that gets thrown away and the time it takes to make the product correctly

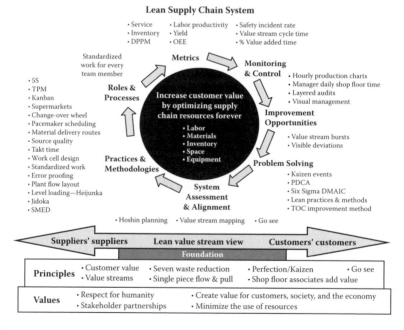

FIGURE 2.5

Lean system.

Taiichi Ohno correctly believed that improving an integrated value stream was the best approach to delivering value to customers and other supply chain participants. Lean has proven its timelessness by delivering results for more than 50 years and remains the best practice for manufacturing plant and supply chain operations.

Implementing the Lean System

The Lean tools for assessment and alignment of an organization's metrics and programs provide a guide for Lean System implementation.

Value Stream Mapping (VSM) is the Lean System assessment and planning tool. (The best resource for learning about this specialized type of process mapping is *Learning to See* by Mike Rother and John Shook from the Lean Enterprise Institute.) VSM includes a standard set of icons and instructions for completing the value stream map. In general, material and information flows are mapped based on actual shop floor observation, creating a map describing the current state of how things are done.

Before actually documenting the current-state VSM, the team must be trained in the basics of the Lean System and Value Stream Mapping. Building a plant value stream map starts with shipping, the process closest to the customer, and follows upstream step-by-step through the receipt of raw materials. Observers note product flow through work centers, key data about each process operation, operator non–value added activities, utilization of material-handling associates, and other signs of the seven waste. Once the current-state value stream map is completed, it is reviewed, information is summarized, and potential value stream improvement projects are noted by placing a starburst at the point in the process where the project would be done.

Before making final decisions on project priorities, a value stream future-state map is developed. The first few times a company does this, we recommend using an experienced coach. There are many possible options when constructing future-state maps, so experience is essential to making correct judgments. It is also usually necessary to have an experienced Lean applications expert train personnel in how these practices work. Decisions about which practice to apply first also require expert judgment based on the specifics of the operation's present condition. Credible Lean experts transfer their knowledge through the combination of classroom and shop floor application. They want their clients to become self-sufficient as quickly as possible.

The future state is constructed by redesigning the value stream using appropriate Lean tools, methodologies, and practices, creating an end-state vision conforming to Lean principles. The future-state and current-state maps are compared, which results in more potential projects. Ninety- and 180-day implementation plans are developed for the projects most important to building the Lean System and improving business results. Because a first priority in Lean implementation is gaining value-stream stability, quick changeover, work cell design for flow, inventory supermarkets, and visual management tools are likely initial projects. This continuous improvement cycle (Figure 2.6) is repeated every 90 to 180 days by going deeper into the value-stream system to standardize, level load, stabilize, and improve flow to a new level.

Each succeeding cycle of improving flow raises a new series of barriers that must be addressed to create continual improvement. This involves taking some level of risk, which potentially disrupts short-term product flow. A fundamental Lean implementation rule is *always protect the customer*. This means that when risk exists, sufficient project resources are applied to ensure that any problems can be dealt with immediately. If issues cannot

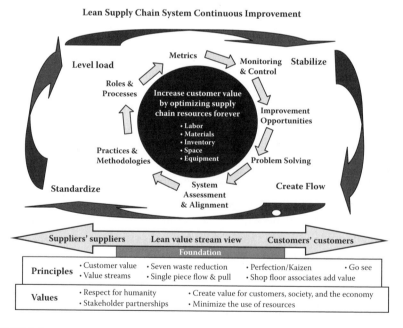

FIGURE 2.6
Lean improvement cycle.

be immediately resolved, additional resources are used to work around problems until they can be resolved.

The Lean Practices

During the last 20 years, Toyota Production System developed myriad practices to expose and solve problems that hampering flow and causing waste. This led to the creation of single piece flow and pull. Resources are optimized in Lean by deploying only those required to support the rate of leveled customer demand.

Lean uses a term called *Takt time*, which defines in seconds the cycle time required to produce a unit of product at a rate sufficient to meet customer demand. It is the drum beat synchronizing all operations and resources. Just enough resources are supplied to meet Takt time, optimizing system resource consumption. Operations are designed to produce at a cycle time slightly lower than Takt time and are synchronized by customer-demand pull signals. Lean practices (see Figure 2.5) allow for quick improvement by their simple application to value stream defects. This array of practices should be applied to the value stream as appropriate through each continuous improvement cycle. (See the Resource Section for specific Lean tools and how to use them.) Lean tools are the means to building, sustaining, and improving the Lean System.

Roles and Processes

Lean standardized work defines Lean System roles for every person in the operation, including management. Implementation starts on the shop floor. Shop floor job activities are classified in three categories: value added, non–value added (waste), and non–value added but required. For example, if the assembly of a product is analyzed, handling of parts is waste, actual assembly is value added, and quality checks are non–value added but required.

A company just beginning its Lean journey typically has only 65 percent of its shop floor operators' time dedicated to value added and non–value added but necessary tasks. This provides an immediate opportunity to improve productivity by 35 percent. Further improvements in productivity are achievable by eliminating or transferring non–valued activities performed by shop floor operators to underutilized material handlers (typically, plant material handlers are only 35 percent utilized). For example, usually in a plant, the forklift truck or powered pallet truck is loaded either going to or returning from the warehouse. This means the percentage of waste related to this activity is at least 50 percent. Standardized work and cell design along with other Lean practices will improve the percentage of value-added time for all shop floor operators.

When we think of standards and standardized work, we automatically think of shop floor operations. Every team member has well-defined standardized work, which is critical to accountability, commitment, building the Lean System, and achievement of results through waste elimination. Standardized work is defined for every level of management including the plant or site manager. Thus, site or plant managers must have structured time in their daily schedules for time on the shop floor. The daily schedule must be arranged so managers review all operations over a defined period. The purpose of this is to

1. audit standardized work,
2. coach team members in the Lean System and continuous improvement,
3. follow up on previously identified deviations to ensure corrective action is being completed, and
4. identify the next level of system improvement.

This is a critical management activity if the Lean System is to be sustained.

The second standardized work activity for plant or site managers is leading policy deployment, or *Hoshin Kanri*, each year to ensure that operations are completely aligned with the annual business plan.

The third standardized work activity for plant managers is conducting regular Lean operational reviews. Regular reviews are required to assure organizational accountability for fulfilling operational plans using Lean continuous improvement.

Metrics

Lean uses metrics to measure results and process effectiveness. Figure 2.5 contains representative high-level metrics. Hoshin planning, also referred to as policy deployment, ensures the selection of the most important metrics in alignment with key customer and business priorities. Metric improvement versus operational plan targets is the focus of regular operational reviews at each organizational level.

Monitoring and Control

Lean is a people-based system, so monitoring and controlling the system relies on management presence on the shop floor. Plant managers audit standardized work previously audited by area managers, completing a cycle of audits completed by every level of leadership.

The first result of these audits is coaching area managers, supervisors, lead people, or shop floor associates about the Lean System, noncompliance, or suggestions for improvement. In Lean, audits are retained and summarized quarterly. One summary is a matrix that includes all the items audited in one manager's operation on one axis of a graph and the auditors' names on the other axis. Ratings are discussed with the entire audit team to maintain calibration between raters.

A second summary is by audit topics across all operations in the facility. This allows the management team to see common weaknesses. Stability of the value stream depends on standardized operational discipline; audits are the control mechanism that maintains system discipline. Lean audits are serious business and included in annual reviews of every associate, team leader, area supervisor, and manager.

Visual management is the Lean System sensing mechanism providing transparency of operational reality and data related to improvement. It also provides clarity of deviations against detailed standards of performance, work procedures, scheduling, inventory, and scrap, among many others. For example, inventory in a supermarket should never be less than the minimum or more than the maximum required. Storage locations in a supermarket are designed to hold the maximum planned inventory. If inventory exceeds the maximum, it must be stored outside the designated location creating a visible variation that will be caught during the daily audit. This allows for immediate follow up in order to understand why the system failed.

Another example is daily review of *day by hour production charts*, which show achievement each hour versus the planned rate. The chart includes the deviation, root cause, and an explanation of the action taken to permanently resolve the problem.

All functions are accountable for responding to shop floor issues so they are quickly resolved. Plant manager daily walks build a healthy tension of joint accountability between the shop floor operator and the plant manager. If the same problems occur repeatedly at a given operation on the shop floor, team members will look to the plant manager to take ownership and resolve the problems. This both creates a healthy tension and reinforces the positive work environment as the plant manager conveys support and respect to shop floor team members, the only people in the plant who truly add value. As a plant's Lean system matures, a more standardized problem–response process follows a well-defined escalation path, ending with the engagement of the plant manager if problems are not resolved within a predetermined time.

Improvement Opportunity Identification and Problem Solving

In summary, Lean tools for identifying improvement opportunities are Value Stream Mapping and visual management. VSM is applied at the Lean System level, where management is responsible for defining and implementing improvements. Visual management on the shop floor drives long-term continuous improvement. Daily deviations are exposed through visual management, and shop floor teams must identify root causes of problems so permanent solutions can be implemented.

The Lean practice for identifying root causes is called *Five Whys*. First, ask why a problem is occurring. The response is then met with a second question: "Why is this occurring?" The process continues with each successive response met with another "why" until the root cause is determined.

Through experience, practitioners have learned it never takes more than five cycles to locate the root cause. After identifying the root cause, the four-step Plan Do Check Act (PDCA) improvement process is applied. This simple method is based on the scientific method taught by Edward Deming. These simple standardized tools allow shop floor team members to learn and apply them. Improvement methodologies, such as Six Sigma and TOC are not well suited for everyday use by shop floor team members because they are more complicated and require significant expert knowledge.

Repeating the Cycle Forever

After completing an initial cycle of Lean System improvement projects and updating the current state, a new future state, which identifies additional improvement projects, must be defined. This process is repeated forever. Simultaneously, the shop floor continuous improvement process is implementing solutions to day-to-day variations. Both follow the same four-step improvement sequence—standardize, level load, stabilize, and create flow—and repeat it continuously, forever.

LEAN Supply Chain System Operational Definition

Definition	An integrated operating system of values, principles, practices, tools, and techniques
Purpose	Increase customer value by optimizing supply chain resources forever
Project Identification	• Future state to current state value stream map gaps • Visible defects
Problem Solving	• Prescriptive practices • PDCA
Performance Measurement	External and internal KPIs
Infrastructure/ Engagement	• Lean expertise • Natural teams • Team leaders

FIGURE 2.7
Lean system operational definition.

Assessing Lean

Lean is a unique operational system (see Figure 2.7) compared with the other methodologies. Toyota, which makes more money each year than all other industry competitors combined and is consistently among the leaders in car reliability and resale value, has been practicing Lean for five decades.

Lean has proven to be a powerful operational model with a great set of tools that eliminate waste and create a sustainable operational system driven by adding value to customers. However, it does not address many important elements needed for a successful supply chain including high-level supply chain design, capacity planning, supply chain competencies, and operational demand planning. Lean is the most powerful operational system known today, but it is just that, a powerful operational system for running and improving the supply chain every day, forever.

THEORY OF CONSTRAINTS

The Theory of Constraints (TOC) was developed by Eli Goldratt and collaborators. It became broadly known in 1984 when Goldratt's book *The Goal* was published. The TOC views an organization as a system with resources linked together to meet the organization's goals.

A *constraint* is a constriction in a system that establishes maximum system output, and all systems have constraints limiting their capacity to improve and better meet or exceed system goals. There are, for example, many types of constraints in a plant—equipment, procedures, policies, manpower, stability of a process, scheduled work time, etc. When looking at a business, sales level may be a constraint. Regardless of which specific constraint exists in a business, resources are always limited. It is critical, therefore, that precious resources are applied to constraints in order to maximize output because working on other improvements that do not resolve constraints will have no effect on increasing the system output.

There are five steps in the TOC improvement process:

1. *Identify the constraint*: What is limiting the system from producing or selling more?
2. *Exploit the constraint*: Get the most out of constrained processes.
3. *Subordinate everything to the constraint:* All resources and activities, including all other operations, must be subordinate to constrained processes.
4. *Elevate the constraint:* Enlarge the capacity of the constrained processes.
5. When the constraint is broken, go to step one and *start over again.*

The Theory of Constraints takes a holistic systems view of all operations of a plant or supply chain. Applied to a business, the TOC purpose is to increase profit. It focuses system improvement on increasing throughput as the best way to add more value. Improvement or elimination of a current constraint results in more throughput, at which point a new system constraint is identified. This continuous cycle drives performance improvement forever. The metrics used in TOC measure the value added produced. Key TOC metrics are

1. T: throughput value of sales less materials cost.
2. I: system's raw material inventory.
3. OE: operating expenses.
4. Dividing T by OE gives a productivity measurement, that is, the rate at which operating expenses are converting raw materials into T.
5. Dividing T by I, the money generated from sales divided by raw material inventory cost, measures inventory turnover.

The TOC includes concepts used to schedule operations. The constrained operation is scheduled in a specific product sequence aligning resource use to meet customer demand. This system drum, which is called Drum Rope Buffer scheduling, sets the pace for all other operations. Upstream, raw materials are subordinated to the constrained operation to make sure materials are available when needed to support the constrained operations schedule. Downstream operations must flow, and are therefore planned and run with sufficient capacity so that all product made by the constrained operation can be processed. Time buffers are used upstream from the constraint so promised shipment dates are met, protecting promise dates from the inevitable process variability. Work is released into production at a rate dictated by the drum and started based on a predetermined total process buffer length. When sales is the constraint, TOC has an approach for solving these problems, which includes use of its problem-solving tools combined with TOC accounting, market segmentation, and pricing strategies to identify what needs to change in order to increase sales. This is a unique feature of the TOC compared with other problem-solving methodologies.

Thinking Process Used to Create and Implement Improvement

TOC is an improvement methodology that supports incremental and breakthrough improvement. Managing the system must include monitoring and controlling the constraint, upstream subordinated processes, and downstream flow processes. This process will identify issues that must be solved in order to maintain and improve system performance. Problems that have no known solution are identified and the TOC three-step process and five tools are applied to provide a solution. It works as follows:

1. What to change?
   Current Reality Tree: The current reality tree is a tool used to identify the root cause of a core problem that has no known solution, in order to eliminate initial undesirable effects. Other undesirable effects related to the original undesirable effect (or defect) are also documented during the process to determine the true core problem.
2. What to change to?
   Evaporating Cloud: The evaporating cloud identifies requirements that the solution must satisfy. The first step is to state the core

problem and define what should replace it. The current core problem exists because it satisfies an organizational need or requirement. This means defined solutions must satisfy needs currently satisfied by whatever caused the core problem and by whatever will replace it.

Future Reality Tree: The future reality tree defines the desirable effects of the solution, which will become the improvement project objectives. Future reality trees create a complete picture of positive and negative consequences of the proposed solution (an idea known as an *injection* in TOC terminology) defined in the evaporating cloud process. Each undesirable effect discovered in making the current reality tree is reviewed to define its opposite or desirable effect. These desirable effects become implementation plan objectives. They are also inputs examined using the prerequisite tree (see below).

The final step is to brainstorm and select an idea that satisfies these needs and has a cause–effect path that will eliminate the core problem.

3. How to change?

Prerequisite tree: The prerequisite tree defines conditions that need to be in place to achieve future reality tree defined objectives. Prerequisite trees ensure all necessary conditions are identified and objectives are set to ensure implementation plans meet them. Projects are implemented efficiently by defining the best sequence to meet these conditions and they are included as input to the transition tree.

Transition tree: The transition tree creates detailed plans to implement the objectives defined in the prerequisite tree. Intermediate objectives and action plans supporting them are delegated to teams or individuals. Teams use transition trees to break down the actions needed to achieve the assigned objectives. These transition tree objectives and actions are used in implementation reviews to ensure overall project objectives are met.

The Theory of Constraints (see Figure 2.8) has two major components, operational system concepts and thinking processes for improvement, and has proven itself a powerful tool for optimizing systems.

Theory of Constraints Operational Definitions

Definition	A methodology that increases systems throughput by optimizing and/or eliminating the constraint
Purpose	Increase enterprise value by improving supply chain throughput, $-T/OE$ and Inventory turns $-T/I$
Project Identification	Identification of the constraint in the system
Problem Solving	TOC thinking process
Performance Measurement	System throughput
Infrastructure/ Engagement	• TOC expertise • Natural teams • Team leaders

FIGURE 2.8
Theory of constraints.

SUPPLY CHAIN OPERATIONS REFERENCE MODEL

The Supply Chain Operations Reference model (SCOR) was developed to aid in understanding, describing, and evaluating supply chains. SCOR differs from Lean and Six Sigma in that it focuses only on evaluation. It identifies the specific best practices needed to improve supply chains, but does not include project implementation strategies because SCOR assumes users have the needed project implementation competencies.

SCOR assessment accomplishes the following:

1. Quickly identifies performance gaps through benchmarking.
2. Eliminates analysis time and effort through predefined cause-and-effect relationships embedded in its three-level logical structure.
3. Provides solutions designed to close performance gaps through best practices.
4. Defines enablers (including IT) required to support best practices.

What is SCOR?

SCOR defines a supply chain as "the integrated processes of Plan, Source, Make, Deliver, and Return spanning from the supplier's supplier to the

SCOR Five Management Processes

"From your supplier's supplier to your customer's customer"
• SCOR Spans
 – All customer interactions, from order entry through paid invoice
 – All physical material transactions, from your supplier's supplier
  to your customer's customer, including

  • Equipment, supplies, spare parts, bulk product, software, etc.
 – All market interactions, from the understanding of aggregate
  demand to the fulfillment of each order

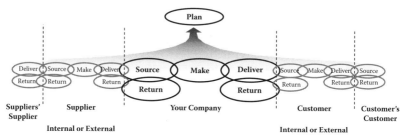

FIGURE 2.9

SCOR scope. (Printed with permission of Supply Chain Council.)

customer's customer" (see Figure 2.9). The key word in this definition is *integrated*. A supply chain isn't defined only by products or only by customers, but needs to consider both views to add value. SCOR is a completely integrated supply chain assessment model with five processes:

Plan: Balancing needs against resources
Source: Processes that connect manufactures to suppliers
Make: Changing the form, fit, or function of something
Deliver: Processes that connect us to our customers (internal and external)
Return: Processes that support the return of products for any reason

The SCOR model breaks down or decomposes its five Level 1 processes into Level 2 and 3 processes (see Figure 2.10). Level 4 defines the specific tasks of Level 3 processes. These tasks are defined to create unique configurations giving a distinctive competitive advantage to a specific business. SCOR contains a Level 4, but it is not included in the model because it is specific to each business, which makes standardization difficult.

Supply chain configuration, meaning, make-to-stock, make-to-order, or engineer-to-order is step one in applying SCOR. This is accomplished using Level 1 and 2 configuration definitions (see Figure 2.11). Configuration is necessary to attain meaningful benchmark data comparisons.

SCOR Process Decomposition Model

Level				
	#	Description	Schematic	Comments
Supply chain operations reference-model	1	Top level (process types)	Source › Make › Deliver / Return	Level 1 defines the scope and content for the supply chain operations reference-model. Basis of competition performance targets are set.
	2	Configuration level (process categories)		A company's supply chain can be "configured-to-order" at level 2 from approximately 17 core "process categories." Companies implement their operations strategy through the configuration they choose for their supply chain.
	3	Process element level (decompose processes)	P3.1 Identify, prioritize, and aggregate production requirements / P3.2 Identify, assess, and aggregate production resources / P3.3 Balance production resources with production requirements / P3.4 Establish detailed production plans	Companies "fine tune" their operations strategy at Level 3. Level 3 defines a company's ability to compete successfully in its chosen markets and consists of • Process element definitions • Process element information inputs and outputs • Process performance metrics • Best practices, where applicable • System capabilities required to support best practices • Systems/tools by vendor
Not in scope	4	Implementation Level (decompose process elements)		Companies implement specific supply-chain management practices at Level 4. Level 4 defines practices to achieve competitive advantage and to adapt to changing business conditions.

FIGURE 2.10

SCOR Process Decomposition Model. (Printed with permission of Supply Chain Council.)

SCOR Level 2 Configuration Toolkit

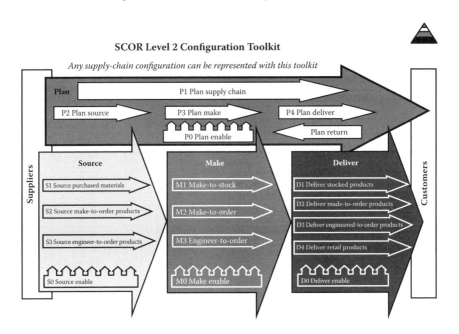

Any supply-chain configuration can be represented with this toolkit

Plan
P1 Plan supply chain
P2 Plan source   P3 Plan make   P4 Plan deliver
P0 Plan enable   Plan return

Suppliers — Source — Make — Deliver — Customers

Source
S1 Source purchased materials
S2 Source make-to-order products
S3 Source engineer-to-order products
S0 Source enable

Make
M1 Make-to-stock
M2 Make-to-order
M3 Engineer-to-order
M0 Make enable

Deliver
D1 Deliver stocked products
D2 Deliver made-to-order products
D3 Deliver engineered-to-order products
D4 Deliver retail products
D0 Deliver enable

FIGURE 2.11

SCOR Level 2 configuration toolkit. (Printed with permission of Supply Chain Council.)

Overview: A SCOR Improvement Project

Once the configuration is complete, current performance is documented using SCOR Level 1 metrics (see Figure 2.12). These metrics are divided into two categories, customer-facing and internal-facing. External benchmarking, using the sources available through the Supply Chain Council, can be done. Measurement comparisons can be done versus peer companies in the same markets or companies from other markets that have leading supply chain practices. Customer-facing metrics are also used to clarify customer expectations by specifying customers' desired supply chain performance.

Performance comparisons identify gaps between the current state and "best in class" benchmarks. Gaps in current performance can also be determined through discussions with key customers.

At this stage, the "to be" state, supply chain performance metric goals that will enhance the business's basis of competition (see Figure 2.13) are defined. Peter Bolsdorf and Robert Rosenbaum, two experienced SCOR practitioners, have written a valuable handbook, *Supply Chain Excellence* (2003), about applying the SCOR process and completing improvement projects. The Supply Chain Council Web site is also an excellent resource for understanding SCOR and available training.

SCOR Level 1 Metrics

Characterize performance from customer-facing and internal-facing perspectives

	Customer-facing		Internal-facing	
SCOR Level 1 **Supply-chain management metrics**	*Reliability &* *responsiveness*	*Agility* *(flexibility)*	*Cost*	*Assets*
Perfect order fulfillment	✓			
Order fulfillment cycle time	✓			
Supply-chain flexibility		✓		
Supply-chain adaptability		✓		
Total supply-chain management cost			✓	
Cost of goods sold			✓	
Cash-to-cash cycle time				✓
Return on supply chain fixed assets				✓

FIGURE 2.12

SCOR Level 1 metrics. (Printed with permission of Supply Chain Council.)

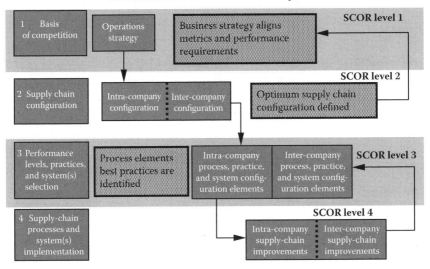

FIGURE 2.13
SCOR improvement process. (Printed with permission of Supply Chain Council.)

The next step is to define specific Level 3 practices that must be changed to achieve these performance goals. Each SCOR level has a set of metrics linked to performance metrics of other levels (see Figures 2.14 and 2.15). Performance goals defined at Level 1 track directly to processes in Level 3, identifying gaps needing change. Performance benchmark comparisons at Level 3 identify specific Level 3 processes that are performing better than, equal to, or worse than benchmark.

Each Level 3 process (see Figure 2.16) is made up of metrics, a series of practices and enabling technology. All three are compared to best practices during benchmarking. Gaps in practices are identified and compared to best practices. The result is clear identification of practices needing change and the definition of new practices. Metrics in Level 1 are linked to Level 2 and 3 metrics. These links ensure implementation of best practices, which will eliminate practice gaps and resolve performance gaps.

This completes the "to be" state. Using SCOR, you can quickly describe supply chain operations from Level 1 down to Level 3. This facilitates the consideration of large chunks of a business by examining supply chain strategy and performance in a top-down fashion. It also identifies strategic and tactical improvement opportunities. SCOR's end-to-end assessment subjugates

Source and Plan Levels 2 and 3 Performance Metrics
Diagnostic Measures Drive Performance Improvement

	Level 2 Performance Metrics				Level 3 Diagnostic Metrics		
	Delivery performance/ quality	Flexibility & responsiveness	Cost	Assets	Supply-chain complexity measures	Supply-chain configuration measures	Supply-chain management practices measures
Plan	• Supply-chain finance and planning costs • Demand/supply planning costs • Inventory days of supply				• % of order changes • # of end devices/ SKUs • Production volume • Inventory carrying cost	• Product volume by channel • # of channels • Supply-chain complexity, # of S/M/D sites	• Planning cycle time • Forecast accuracy • Obsolete/end of life inventory days of supply • Replan cycle • Order entry methods • Order entry modes
Source	• Material acquisition costs • Source cycle time • Raw material DOS				• % purchasing spending by distance • # of suppliers	• Purchased material by geography • % of purchasing spending by distance	• Supplier delivery performance • Payment period • % part numbers received with lead time <8 weeks • % unpenalized 30-day decrease

FIGURE 2.14

SCOR Source and Plan Level 2 and 3 performance metrics. (Printed with permission of Supply Chain Council.)

Make and Deliver Levels 2 and 3 Performance Metrics
Diagnostic Measures Drive Performance Improvement

	Level 2 Performance Metrics				Level 3 Diagnostic Metrics		
	Delivery performance/ quality	Flexibility & responsiveness	Cost	Assets	Supply-chain complexity measures	Supply-chain configuration measures	Supply-chain management practices measures
Make	• # of returns/complaints • Build order attainment • Make cycle time • Product quality				• # of devices/SKUs • Upside production flexibility	• Manufacturing process steps by geography • Asset turns	• Value-add % • % build-to-stock, % build-to-order • % of mfg. order changes due to internal issues • WIP & plant FG DOS
Deliver	• Fill rates • Order management costs • Order fulfillment lead time • Forecast accuracy by channel				• # of orders, line items, & shipments by channel • % parts returned • % re-returns	• Delivery locations by geography • # of channels • Field & samples FG DOS	• Published delivery lead time • # of faultless invoices

FIGURE 2.15

SCOR Make and Deliver Level 2 and 3 performance metrics. (Printed with permission of Supply Chain Council.)

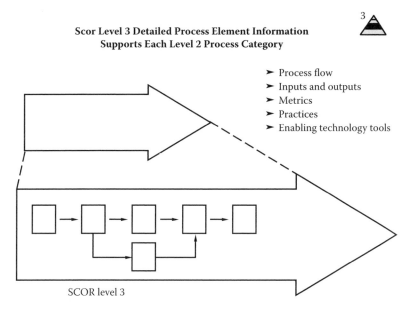

FIGURE 2.16
SCOR Level 3 process elements. (Printed with permission of Supply Chain Council.)

organizational structure and its "silos" by examining processes from a customer's perspective. SCOR can be used to describe virtually any supply chain, whether training employees to make ice cream or launch the space shuttle.

BARRIERS TO IMPLEMENTATION

Understanding the evolution and demonstrated success of improvement methods raises some hard questions:

1. Why are top manufacturing and services business leaders, who need every operational improvement possible, not demanding immediate implementation of these proven methodologies in their organizations?

   • The single biggest barrier is a lack of supply chain understanding by business leaders. Lack of a common framework, language, assessment, and improvement tools makes understanding supply chain difficult and few have learned this from their career experience.

- Poor implementation of improvement methodologies is another cause of slow deployment. Many times failure leads to excuses; for example, "the methodology doesn't work in our business." There are many reasons why the implementation fails, but it is never the fault of the methodology. It is more likely a failure of leadership.

2. Why do very good companies not have their supply chains designed and fully aligned to deliver their value proposition every day?

- Most companies are managed in "silos" and focus on operational excellence of the pieces—sourcing, manufacturing, logistics—rather than the end-to-end supply chain.
- Strategy in most businesses stops with sales, marketing, and product development. There is little time spent ensuring alignment of operations to deliver performance required for business strategy success.
- Most companies fail to develop their own version of the Toyota Production System. This means they are missing an opportunity to focus on improvement of their system as a whole. As a result, they have an operational system for every plant, which results in time wasted deciding how things should be done at each one.

3. Why hasn't a common language and methodology for supply chain assessment been adopted?

- The curriculum in business schools is inadequate and frequently doesn't provide significant understanding of operations management.
- Professors fall into the same trap as practitioners; they become familiar with one improvement methodology, teach it, and believe it is superior to the others.
- Supply chain consulting companies convince customers that their unique methodology adds value and have no interest in adopting a common assessment framework and methodology.

4. Why is the adoption of proven best practices so slow?

- Consultants attempt to extend the life of a particular methodology by integrating tools from "competing" methodologies, creating new labels, and proclaiming the result is the integration of the two methodologies. An example of this is Lean Six Sigma: A consultant integrates selective Lean tools into his or her problem-solving approach and calls it Lean, disregarding the fact that Lean is an operational system.

- Adopters and consultants focus only on tools to solve specific problems and neglect to integrate the true purpose and principles of improvement methodologies into their company cultures, for example, by applying Lean System's tools to solve specific problems without understanding their underlying purpose, which is to build an end-to-end supply chain system. The Lean System is an operational supply chain platform with continuous improvement inherently built into the system. Applying Lean tools without this understanding may produce short-term gains but no sustainable long-term transformational improvement.

- Software market leaders also contribute to slow adoption of best practices by continuing to sell their products with the implied promise that customers are getting the latest best practices embedded in their products. An example is the Lean pull system. Only recently have major enterprise resource planning (ERP) software suppliers begun to integrate electronic pull signal capability into their systems. Pressure from customers and small startups with pull system functionality has led big ERP players to start supporting electronic Kanban. It is a beginning, but not sufficient to support a Lean operational system.

- Myriad voices advocating various solutions and views of supply chain are another part of the problem. Lean, Six Sigma, TOC, and SCOR are being used by companies to improve competitiveness but are implemented separately, for example, by different departments or different plants. As a result, there is often friction among the groups advocating each methodology.

- Advocates, who proclaim their position, view, and methodology as the "right one" and insist anyone serious about improvement must adopt it, limit progress.

Business leaders will take decisive action when an improvement strategy and methodology can be effectively deployed based on proven results. The next chapter provides a comparative analysis of the various improvement methodologies and their convergence into a Sustainable Improvement Roadmap.

REFERENCES

Bolsdorf, Peter, and Robert Rosenbaum. *Supply chain excellence*. New York: Amacom, 2003.

Goldratt, Eli, and Jeff Cox. *The goal*. Great Barrington, MA: North River Press, 1984.

Ohno, Taiichi. *Toyota production system: Beyond large-scale production*. Cambridge, MA: Productivity Press, 1988.

Rother, Mike, and John Shook. *Learning to see*. Cambridge, MA: Lean Enterprise Institute, 2003.

Schonberger, Richard. *Japanese manufacturing techniques*. New York: Free Press, 1982.

Womack, James P., Daniel T. Jones, and Daniel Roos. *The machine that changed the world*. New York: Rawson Associates, 1990.

3

Sustainable Improvement Roadmap Comparing Continuous Improvement Strategies

---

Business leaders need a holistic continuous improvement strategy and methodology that assesses the end-to-end supply chain and supplies tools and practices for improving all capabilities in light of their business's priorities. Lean, Six Sigma, TOC (Theory of Constraints), and SCOR (Supply Chain Operations Reference model) have produced good results that have contributed to improving competitiveness, but they do not always create long-term, end-to-end sustainable supply chain improvement.

Is it possible these approaches are all good, but individually none of them represents the optimum solution to sustainable operational competitiveness? Are they conflicting or complementary? Can they be used together in a way that is more powerful than using them alone? Are there some gaps that remain unfilled even using all of these methodologies?

Before jumping to conclusions, we need to define the criteria and attributes a proposed solution would contain. The following criteria would ensure the supply chain operational performance necessary to enable a sustainable market leading position. The solution would be

1. designed and operated to deliver the business's value proposition,
2. operated across all participants from suppliers to customers optimizing total supply chain added value,
3. designed and operated with known best practices to ensure competitive excellence,

4. connected to customers' definition of value added and able to adapt to changing customer and market needs, and

5. improved continuously at a rate faster than that of key competitors, using maximum organizational potential ensuring a sustainable competitive advantage.

What would be the attributes of a supply chain improvement process that delivers supply chains meeting these criteria? All of the methodologies summarized in Chapter 2 have strengths and limitations. By synthesizing these methodologies, the strengths of one can be examined against the limitations of another to see if the convergence of these methodologies can remedy all identified limitations. This process constructs the mosaic of a converged methodology, resulting in a robust process capable of sustainable results. It creates a Sustainable Improvement Roadmap (SIR).

SCOR: STRENGTHS AND LIMITATIONS

SCOR has much to contribute to the Sustainable Improvement Roadmap, but it has certain limitations as well (see Figure 3.1).

Strengths

SCOR is a top-down approach to supply chain assessment with a holistic business view of the entire supply chain and its processes. This ensures assessment outcomes linked to the business's competitive basis. External benchmarking provides a business with a fact-based reality check of its operational competitiveness. Benchmark-quantified performance gaps provide the basis for a business case connected to true root causes through the multilevel decomposition model, thus increasing assessment credibility. An end-state vision is created through a "to be" state, which drives project selection priorities ensuring improvement projects that improve the entire system.

In sum, SCOR's standardized language and supply chain assessment methodology offer numerous advantages including

SCOR

Operational Definition		Strengths and Limitations
		SCOR Strengths
Definition	End to end supply chain assessment methodology using metrics, benchmarking, process decomposition models and best practices	• Top-down approach
		• Scope includes the entire supply chain
		• Enables supply chain performance and practice benchmarking
		• Focus on value creation for customers
		• End state driven project selection
Purpose	Design and improve supply chains by applying known best practices	• Supply chain level metrics for system performance
		• Enables business case development
		• Includes all the processes
		• Establishes a common language and tools
Project Identification	Disconnects, process & practice gaps	• Internal and external supply chain metrics
		• Metric and activity alignment across organizational boundaries
		• Continuous regeneration of improvement opportunities
		• Aligns all supply chain activities with customer and competitive requirements
Problem Solving	Prescriptive best practices	• Prescriptive best practice identified
		SCOR Limitations
Performance Measurement	External and internal KPI's	• Top-down approach
		• Assessment only process
		• Doesn't build companywide operational processes
		• Superficial top management understanding
Infrastructure/ Engagement	SCOR expertise supply chain knowledge	• Lack of process definition for managing supply chain collaboration
		• Lack of process definition for execution management processes
		• Lack of scientific problem solving to improve unit operations performance—yields, run times, quality, etc.
		• Not fully aligned with Lean metrics

FIGURE 3.1
SCOR: Operational definition, strengths and limitations.

- a reality check on operational excellence,
- assessments that are easy to integrate into annual strategic planning processes,
- assistance in competitive analysis because understanding financial performance of competitors can be linked to advantageous or disadvantageous process areas,
- a financial business case that is easily built from Level 1 benchmarked data, and
- a long-term sustainable operational competitive advantage that can be built through continued assessment process use.

Internal and external metrics link business requirements to total supply chain operations across all functional boundaries. Linked multilevel

SCOR metrics ensure relevance and alignment of operational metrics across organizations and programs to improve supply chains.

Limitations

SCOR is an assessment process, so it has no capability to resolve core operational issues such as run time, yield, or quality defects. Its top-down process does not fully engage an organization in assessment, project selection, or implementation. This implies that it can be an important component of building a continuous improvement culture in a business, but the lack of full organizational engagement makes it difficult to capture all business team members' minds and hearts. Without full organizational engagement, the continuous improvement potential of a business will never be achieved. Business leaders relate to Level 1 performance metrics and benchmarking, but few have enough desire to understand SCOR at a deeper level. This does not mean it can't be effective, but using SCOR as a primary component of strategic planning is difficult to achieve.

Finally, SCOR was launched in 1996, and much has been learned since then about improving supply chain performance. Lack of deep relationships or collaboration processes is a gap in SCOR. It treats these as an enabling process. (An enabling process is a prerequisite for the success of an operational process.) In the case of SCOR, the plan is the operational process; the collaboration of participants enables the best practices of the plan process. This is logical but doesn't recognize that collaboration is no longer restricted to planning. The highest performing supply chains are interconnected operationally, as when kanban signals from one company automatically generate replenishment from another. Cost targets and projects that are done collaboratively between customers and their suppliers are other examples of the types of common collaboration.

One only has to examine the PRTM maturity model to understand the overall performance and magnitude of shared benefit collaboration among all supply chain participants. (PRTM is a management consulting group. For in-depth information about the PRTM model, see Cohen and Roussel, 2005.) It is fair to conclude that collaboration is a supply chain's brain and nerve system and not simply an enabling process for planning. Doug Lambert's book *Supply Chain Management* (2004) does an excellent job of defining collaboration processes, their importance, and how to segment participants to achieve effective collaboration.

Another gap in SCOR is the lack of direct metric alignment and support for Lean. In the Lean world, traditional terms such as *schedule attainment* have no meaning. Every schedule in a Lean System is a market-generated pull, whether it is a make-to-stock, make-to-order, or engineer-to-order schedule. Lean is both the proven best operational system known today and the operational execution best practice.

SCOR still contains references to metrics for schedule attainment, an obsolete concept because no rationale exists for planning system-generated orders. Because Lean replenishment methods respond to actual demand, there are no forecast-based replenishment orders to fill. What matters is compliance with pull signals and loop times for replenishing supermarkets.

This leads to another SCOR process gap. The last ten years have brought great understanding about managing execution. The concept that execution is a subset of planning is obsolete because planning systems should provide the proper state of readiness based on execution system parameters. Since planning systems should not launch orders, what could be the logic for continuing the current thinking?

Another high-level process called *Execution* should be added to the current Plan, Source, Make, Deliver, and Return processes. The Execution process is a "twin" to the Plan process and not simply a Plan process enabler. The Execution process dynamically uses real-time events to manage execution across the other five Level 1 SCOR processes. It is sales and operations planning on steroids, not simply reacting to events but sensing events early enough to take preventive actions such as changing plans or planning parameters so a negative consequence is avoided. Military leaders often say, even perfect plans become out of date once the first shot is fired; this is also true in business. Execution is essential to supply chain competitive advantage; it can't be treated as a subset of the Level 1 Plan process.

It is understood today that execution management and planning excellence are equally important for success. The planning-dominant paradigm era is over and supply chain tools for assessment and design must also change from planning-based supply chain management to execution-based supply chain management.

LEAN: STRENGTHS AND LIMITATIONS

Lean is a holistic supply chain operational system best practice with imbedded continuous improvement capability linked to customer value (see Figure 3.2).

Strengths

Value stream future-state mapping creates an end-state system designed to drive the right process improvement, adding value to customers and improving business results. The repetitive cycle of standardize, level load, stabilize, and create flow ensures continuous regeneration of improvement opportunities as perfection is pursued.

Hoshin kanri (policy deployment) ensures complete alignment of metrics and projects across the organization connecting their efforts to business priorities. Lean's easily understood standard practices lead to fast gains as time is not used in developing a new solution.

Problem solving in lean is a combination of prescriptive standard practices and scientific problem solving. This allows for development of new

LEAN System

Operational Definitions		Strengths and Limitations
		Lean Strengths
Definition	An integrated operating system of values, principles, practices, tools, and techniques	• Scope is all operational supply chain processes
		• Focus on value creation for customers
		• Builds companywide operational system
Purpose	Increase customer value by optimizing supply chain resources forever	• End-state driven project selection
		• Regenerates opportunity forever
		• Metric and activity alignment across organizational boundaries
Project Identification	• Future state to current state value stream map gaps	• Prescriptive best practice solutions
	• Visible defects	• Scientific problem-solving method
		• Total organizational involvement
		• Establishes common language and tools
Problem Solving	• Prescriptive practices	• Builds continuous improvement culture
	• PDCA	**Lean Limitations**
Performance Measurement	External and internal KPI's	• Top management understanding is superficial
		• Difficult to scale
		• Rigor can suffer without management engagement
Infrastructure/ Engagement	• Lean expertise	• Difficult to tie to the bottom line at the start
	• Natural teams	• Includes only operational processes
	• Team leaders	

FIGURE 3.2

Lean: Operational definition, strengths and limitations.

solutions when no existing Lean prescriptive solution applies. Lean engages the entire organization in improvement and places shop floor operators at the system's center, so continuous improvement is part of everyone's job. Finally, Lean builds a continuous improvement system and culture with a common language, tools, goals, and objectives.

Limitations

Top management normally finds Lean difficult to understand. Taiichi Ohno (1988) didn't approve of written documentation about the Toyota Production System development. He considered it a waste of time and instructed his engineers to spend their time on the shop floor improving operations.

There is much tacit knowledge in Lean because it evolved through practice and has been passed down through verbal sharing of experience (Womack et al., 1989). Only recently could Lean be explained by a set of principles and concepts that tie its practices together into a system. This has made understanding Lean quite difficult. It is like trying to understand the entire universe by looking through a telescope that can focus on only one star at a time.

A broader perspective was needed to facilitate understanding Lean's wide variety of processes and tools (Womack et al., 1989). Lean is not easily scaled up. The fastest complete systems implementations take two to three years, as an organization absorbs an immense amount of specific knowledge and applies it to its value streams. Building a team of internal Lean experts also takes two to three years before members have implemented all Lean system practices, and even then, they have achieved only a novice status as Lean coaches.

The third limitation is reliance on committed shop floor management time to sustain gains and to lead the next level of improvement. This requires commitment from the entire organization to support the dedicated time needed by plant or supply chain leaders to make Lean successful. It also takes enlightened financial leadership to either change some of the financial operational measurements or educate their organizations on how to look at financial benefits created by Lean. Sometimes the early results from Lean are difficult to tie to the bottom line. For example, the freeing up of space in a plant, which occurs early in implementation, is not necessarily viewed as a financial benefit. Unless there is a need for more equipment to make the product ready for sale, this space is not valued in traditional financial systems. Another example is inventory reduction. This improvement in working capital will likely cause a short-term reduction in output, which will reflect negatively on factory costs or cost of goods as a percentage of sales metrics. This takes some faith from top management. Results will start coming in year one, but financial metrics of the business may not show positive gains during the first six months.

Last, Lean includes only operational processes and not other required processes, such as supply chain network design, planning processes for materials and capacity planning, and tools to solve complex multivariable process problems. Lean needs to be supported by these processes, but it doesn't actually define network design or materials and capacity planning processes. However, none of this detracts from the observable fact that Lean is the world's best operational system known today.

SIX SIGMA: STRENGTHS AND LIMITATIONS

Six Sigma is project centric, focusing on the resolution of specific defects in order to provide measurable business benefits (see Figure 3.3).

Strengths

Six Sigma should measure only hard savings, cost, or cash benefits actually tracked to an operating budget, inventory, accounts payable, or accounts receivable balance. This assures that some true net financial benefit will show up in the profit and loss statement. Six Sigma creates a companywide improvement methodology allowing salaried team members to engage in problem solving, maximizing their improvement capacity.

Six Sigma requires investment in an infrastructure of experts for implementation and ongoing support. Because training is focused on deployment of the tool set, it is relatively easy to scale up quickly.

Six Sigma's fact-based problem-solving rigor gives a good level of confidence that true root causes are being addressed, and creates data-based thinking throughout the organization.

Buy-in with respect to projects solutions is created using an acceptance strategy that is part of the implementation process. This is accomplished through the use of tools such as stakeholder and force field analysis.

Six Sigma

Operational Definitions		Strengths and Limitations
Definition	A structured improvement methodology using a standard approach and statistical tools	**Six Sigma Strengths** • Scope is specific process defects reduction • Establishes a common language and tools • Easily scalable • Scientific problem-solving method
Purpose	Reduce process variability	• Bottom-line oriented • Top management relates to it easily
Project Identification	Keys issues or process problems	• Control plan to keep the gains • Acceptance strategy and tools
Problem Solving	Prescriptive DMAIC problem-solving method	**Six Sigma Limitations** • Scope is specific process defects reduction
Performance Measurement	Specific process and project metrics	• Potential for KPI disconnect • Lack of clear connection to best system improvements • No prescriptive solutions
Infrastructure/ Engagement	• Six Sigma expertise • MBB/BB/GB resources • Ad hoc teams	• Bottoms-up opportunity generation • Limited engagement of the shop floor team members • Runs out of high value projects • Doesn't build a continuous improvement culture

FIGURE 3.3
Six Sigma: Operational definition, strengths and limitations.

Rigorous control plans are established as a part of finalizing projects to ensure improvements become permanent and bottom-line business benefits are realized. In addition to direct financial benefits, Six Sigma develops leaders and contributes positively to company culture. The common language and toolset facilitates cross-functional projects and improved problem solving and team skills throughout the organization.

Six Sigma's final strength is that its project focus, measurable defect elimination, and direct financial benefits are easily understood by the business's leadership and aligned with their need to meet the annual business objectives.

Limitations

Six Sigma identifies projects that resolve known process defects and variations or gaps between current performance and the requirements of the operating plan. What Six Sigma doesn't have is assessment tools that look at overall supply chain or plant processes to continuously generate opportunities and connect improvements to the entire system. A good example is the common use of Material Requirements Planning (MRP) systems for forecasting, planning, and order generation.

Six Sigma could be used to fix specific defects that occur in forecasting, planning, and order generation, but it is not designed to challenge the *push planning* concepts that are the basis of MRP systems. This leads to two issues: (1) Systemwide assessment of projects can't be done to ensure that projects with the best total system impact receive the highest priority, and (2) projects may be implemented that have a positive impact on one step in the process, but an offsetting effect on another process.

Six Sigma programs normally train only salaried personnel, leaving shop floor team members feeling excluded. An opportunity to engage the entire organization in continuous improvement is therefore missed.

Six Sigma organizational infrastructure can also lead to a rigid and exclusive view of continuous improvement. Corporate Six Sigma organizations have a tendency to force-fit every other improvement methodology into the DMAIC (define, measure, analyze, improve, control) framework. There is nothing wrong with the inclusion of Lean tools, for example, in the Six Sigma toolkit. What is wrong is selling this combined solution as Lean or Lean Six Sigma, implying that this captures the real essence and purpose of Lean. This distortion contributes to the difficulty business leaders have in understanding the various improvement methodologies available and their relative value.

Six Sigma has no process or tools for ensuring complete alignment of metrics and projects across the entire organization. Goal trees, also called Y-trees, are used to align projects with business goals. This isn't effective in assuring alignment of metrics across organizations nor in prioritizing projects to meet the metrics. This can lead to less than optimum results at minimum, and potentially projects that serve one function well while not contributing to overall business improvement.

Six Sigma solutions are developed during each project because prescriptive solutions are not a part of Six Sigma. This is one reason for projects taking months to reach fruition, as solutions have to be identified, developed, tested, and then implemented. Even using shared project databases and encouraging replication of solutions are minimally effective in creating prescriptive solutions.

Finally, the assessment tools, which continually regenerate high-value projects, are missing in Six Sigma. A few years of eliminating low-hanging fruit results in a declining number of Black Belt projects, making return on infrastructure investment more difficult to justify.

LEARNED FROM EXPERIENCE: PAUL

LEAN GIVES AN ORGANIZATION NEW EYES WITH WHICH TO SEE OPPORTUNITIES TO IMPROVE

For five years, 3M saw tremendous improvements in cost, quality, and service. By the fifth year, it became more challenging to identify big-impact projects with significant financial benefits. Six Sigma needed a shot in the arm: a new approach to continue filling project hoppers with significant projects. Lean brought a new way to look at our value streams and helped us identify big new improvement opportunities, refilling our project hoppers and continuing significant progress.

THEORY OF CONSTRAINTS: STRENGTHS AND LIMITATIONS

TOC is a top–down improvement methodology that defines the entire business as the scope of the system to be improved (see Figure 3.4).

Strengths

The heart of the methodology is the focus on the system constraint, which ensures that all resources are applied to maximize the system improvement benefit.

Systems always have constraints to be eliminated, so TOC will always regenerate opportunities for improvement. Markets and customers eventually become the constraint when there is more capacity available than the amount of product the organization is currently able to sell. This places the customer at the center as the constraint.

The TOC thinking process is based on the scientific method; that is, it identifies the root cause(s) of a problem and develops effective solutions. The thinking process is useful for making incremental and breakthrough improvements. The TOC methodology also provides a set of concepts for building a plant or supply chain's order scheduling and flow control processes.

Theory of Constraints

Operational Definitions		Strengths and Limitations
Definition	A methodology that increases systems throughput by optimizing and/or eliminating the constraint	**TOC Strengths** • Top-down driven • Focuses improvement on the constraint • Regenerates opportunity forever
Purpose	Increase enterprise value by optimizing supply chain throughput, T/I, and T/OE	• Scientific problem-solving method • Breakthrough improvement method • Concepts to build the operational order scheduling and control system
Project Identification	Identification of the constraint in the system	• Easy to tie to the bottom line
Problem Solving	TOC thinking process	• Concepts to increase market share when it is the constraint
Performance Measurement	System throughput	**TOC Limitations** • Top management understanding • Limited tools and practices to build the operational system
Infrastructure/ engagement	• TOC expertise • Natural teams • Team leaders	• Complex unique language • Limited engagement of the shop floor team members

FIGURE 3.4
Theory of constraints: strengths and limitations.

Limitations

The unique language and thinking process of the TOC is not readily understood by top management, which is a barrier to its effective use across the enterprise. The entire company leadership team must be on board in leading the use of TOC across the company because at some point in the journey the constraint will move to all the operating functions in the organization. If TOC is applied only in manufacturing and the supply chain without total organizational involvement, maximum potential benefit will not be achieved.

It also takes enlightened financial leadership to change some of the financial operational measurements or educate the organization on how to look at the financial benefits created by TOC. Becoming proficient in applying TOC takes time, again, because the language and rigorous improvement methodology are not easily understood.

TOC thinking provides no prescriptive solutions but rather a very rigorous scientific method problem-solving process. It ensures focus on the most important defect, the real problem is well understood, root causes are defined, and implementation will treat all the root causes and mitigate any unintended consequences.

The TOC process and language complexity along with the top-down nature of TOC is not conducive to engaging the shop floor. The TOC thinking process has great merit and is unique; on the other hand, the use of TOC concepts to design the operational system has no unique value. The depth and rigor of the Lean System is more robust and satisfies the design objectives of Drum Buffer Rope; it just does it in a different way.

TOC thinking should be applied when analyzing value stream maps to make sure the right things are being improved. The thinking process should be included in the improvement tools for root cause analysis, and TOC should be the tool of choice when a breakthrough is needed.

SUSTAINABLE IMPROVEMENT ROADMAP

With an understanding of strengths and weaknesses of SCOR, Lean, Six Sigma, and TOC, one has to ask the following:

- Can these methodologies be used together to create a more robust business improvement methodology?
- Can a Sustainable Improvement Roadmap (SIR) be defined that doesn't try to force-fit these powerful methodologies into one another, but creates a new improvement approach that applies each system's collective strengths to create a more powerful continuous improvement methodology?

The Sustainable Improvement Roadmap's attributes are drawn from the collective strengths of current improvement methodologies. In addition, the capability needed to mitigate any remaining limitations is identified. This provides the opportunity for innovations in continuous improvement methodologies.

Figure 3.5 summarizes the improvement methodologies' collective strengths and limitations. Strengths and limitations that mitigate each other are grouped at the top (see column headed "Strengths That Mitigate Limitations"). At the bottom of the left column, additional collective strengths are enumerated. Some specific methodology strengths were not included as they apply to only a particular methodology and don't

Summary of Strengths and Unmitigated Limitations

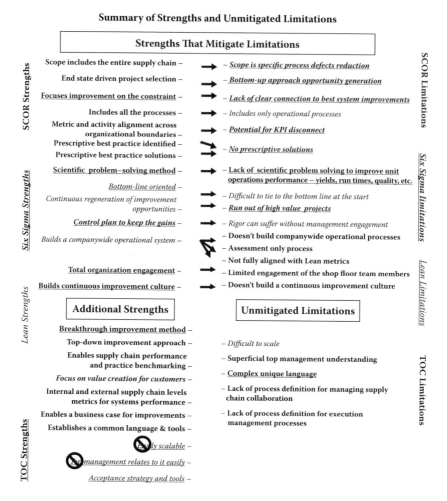

Strengths That Mitigate Limitations

SCOR Strengths		SCOR Limitations
Scope includes the entire supply chain –	→	– *Scope is specific process defects reduction*
End state driven project selection –	→	– *Bottom-up approach opportunity generation*
Focuses improvement on the constraint –	→	– *Lack of clear connection to best system improvements*
Includes all the processes –	→	– *Includes only operational processes*
Metric and activity alignment across organizational boundaries –	→	– *Potential for KPI disconnect*
Prescriptive best practice identified – Prescriptive best practice solutions –	→ →	– *No prescriptive solutions*

Six Sigma Strengths — Six Sigma limitations

- Scientific problem–solving method – → – Lack of scientific problem solving to improve unit operations performance – yields, run times, quality, etc.
- *Bottom-line oriented –*
- *Continuous regeneration of improvement opportunities –* → – *Difficult to tie to the bottom line at the start* → – *Run out of high value projects*
- *Control plan to keep the gains –* → – *Rigor can suffer without management engagement*
- *Builds a companywide operational system –* – **Doesn't build companywide operational processes**
- – Assessment only process
- – Not fully aligned with Lean metrics
- Total organization engagement – → – Limited engagement of the shop floor team members
- Builds continuous improvement culture – → – Doesn't build a continuous improvement culture

Lean Strengths — Lean Limitations

Additional Strengths

Breakthrough improvement method –

Top-down improvement approach –

Enables supply chain performance and practice benchmarking –

Focus on value creation for customers –

Internal and external supply chain levels metrics for systems performance –

Enables a business case for improvements –

Establishes a common language & tools –

~~ly scalable –~~

~~management relates to it easily –~~

Acceptance strategy and tools –

Unmitigated Limitations

– *Difficult to scale*

– Superficial top management understanding

– Complex unique language

– Lack of process definition for managing supply chain collaboration

– Lack of process definition for execution management processes

TOC Strengths — TOC Limitations

FIGURE 3.5
Strengths and limitations.

mitigate limitations of other methodologies. An example is the ease of scalability of Six Sigma, which doesn't mitigate the difficulty of scaling Lean across an enterprise. At the bottom of the right column, limitations that have not been mitigated are listed. Some unmitigated limitations must be recognized and addressed when applying SIR to ensure success. These limitations serve to identify needs for future continuous improvement methodology innovation.

Resolving the Unmitigated Limitations

The five unmitigated limitations of SIR are as follows:

1. It is difficult to scale.
2. There is superficial top management understanding.
3. It has a complex unique language.
4. There is a lack of execution management process definition.
5. There is a lack of supply chain collaboration process definition.

Difficult to Scale

The Sustainable Improvement Roadmap elements are difficult to scale because they are transformative processes and practices. Six Sigma, TOC, and SCOR, with leadership commitment including infrastructure investment, can be scaled up across the entire organization, rapidly producing very significant savings in the first year.

Lean operations transformation can't be taught and applied across an entire organization, like Six Sigma, because it relies on gaining bottom-up understanding and engagement. This is not a weakness of Lean, just recognition of a reality. Lean requires time to mature to institutionalize powerful cultural change. This cultural change depends on aligning the entire management structure's thinking and action, a formidable task that requires persistence and time. It takes two to three years with complete commitment to achieve a mature Lean operational system in a plant. The only solution to the difficulty of scaling Lean is the absolute commitment of top leadership along with sufficient dedicated resources to minimize Lean System maturation time.

Superficial Top Management Understanding

Business leaders need a level of supply chain understanding in order to be an effective implementation champion. There is no substitute for investing the time necessary to learn a better approach and way of managing the total operations improvement of the business.

Complex Unique Language

Only TOC's problem-solving process uses a complex and unique language that takes time to understand, much less apply. Unless a person intends to routinely use the TOC problem-solving approach, it is best to locate a trained practitioner who has used the TOC method many times.

Lack of Execution Management Process Definition

There is strong empirical evidence disproving the assumption that execution is simply an extension of planning. This view has dominated ever since MRP became a common approach in the late 1970s.

The Toyota Production System provided the first evidence that the scheduling process should not be linked to planning and execution processes. For four decades, since the Toyota Production System introduced the pull system, it has proven itself the best way to schedule. Scheduling is not an extension of planning; rather *actual* sales to customers trigger schedules. All supply chain operations are synchronized by a set of pull systems not triggered by planning systems.

A planning system has a very important role in ensuring resources are in place to support execution. It should bring issues needing action to the surface and support the effective balance of supply resources and demand variability, but it should not be used to trigger or manage execution.

The plan should establish and maintain demand-related inventory control parameters to increase or decrease finished goods inventory when future events indicate changes are needed.

The second evidence that scheduling should not be linked to planning and execution processes is the increasing use of dynamic execution management processes and tools. The planning process establishes the parameters within which operations are expected to meet service, quality, and cost objectives, for example, customer demand level. The planning process establishes the top and bottom boundaries within which the operations are expected to flex while meeting operational objectives. These boundaries reflect an operation's flexibility and response capability, which have been designed into these boundaries. When demand goes outside the top boundary, action must be taken immediately to prevent a customer service failure. Materials must be expedited, additional overtime approved, people hired, shifts added, and outsourcing partners used. The point is that none of this directly involves the planning system, as its role is to provide the state of preparedness. Execution management is a Level 1 process that should be positioned side by side with the Plan process in SCOR. In their book *Strategic Supply Chain Management*

(2005), Cohen and Roussel provide an example from Seagate Technology to demonstrate this point. Seagate is dynamically managing order fulfillment based on orders from customers by utilizing many IT suppliers to support dynamic demand and supply management. Companies will have to define their own processes and practices until more published content is available.

Lack of Supply Chain Collaboration Process Definition

The thinking and evolving practices of collaboration across supply chains is beyond the ability of current methodologies such as SCOR. SCOR treats collaboration as an extension of planning, defining it as a best practice. Planning collaboration is certainly a component of collaboration, but it is not all of collaboration. Collaboration includes execution, product development, and internal communication to successfully meet business goals.

SCOR processes need to be updated to add collaboration as a Level 1 process reflecting today's reality. Collaboration can't be treated as simply an enabling process element within Plan, Source, Make, Deliver, and Return processes. There is valuable work going on that is beginning to develop operational processes definitions.

In *Strategic Supply Chain Management*, Cohen and Roussel provide valuable insight into the importance of collaboration in describing PRTM's Supply Chain Maturity Model. The model makes clear that collaboration is as important as practice excellence in the total value gained by supply chain participants. Other important work involving collaboration has been done by Doug Lambert of Supply Chain Forum. In the first edition (2004) of Doug's book *Supply Chain Management*, the collaboration process is defined. In the second edition (2005), Doug provides collaboration assessment tools to identify improvement opportunities. In the next few years, more detailed process definitions and best practices will become available, but until then companies will have to use the information available to define their own approach to collaboration.

Attributes of the Sustainable Improvement Roadmap: Strengths and Solutions for the Unmitigated Limitations

Five criteria defined at the beginning of this chapter are supported by attributes of SIR. SIR integrates the best of current methodologies and provides direction for filling the remaining gaps. Sustainable operational competitive leadership is achievable through consistent and long-term SIR deployment.

1. Designed and operated to deliver the business's value proposition.
   - Internal and external supply chain–level metrics for systems performance
   - Top-down improvement approach
   - Builds a companywide operational system
   - Bottom-line oriented
   - Metric and activity alignment across organizational boundaries

2. Operated across all participants from suppliers to customers optimizing total supply chain added value.
   - Scope includes the entire supply chain
   - Includes all processes
   - Supports end-to-end collaboration
   - Dynamic execution management process

3. Designed and operated with known best practices to ensure competitive excellence.

4. Connected to customers' definition of value added and able to adapt to changing customer and market needs.
   - Focuses on value creation for customers
   - Enables supply chain performance and practice benchmarking

5. Improved continuously at the maximum potential of the organization to ensure sustainable competitive advantage.
   - Enables a business case for improvements
   - Establishes a common language and toolset
   - Includes an acceptance strategy and tools
   - Contains a breakthrough improvement method
   - Builds a continuous improvement culture
   - Engages the total organization
   - Establishes control plans to keep the gains
   - Continuously regenerates improvement opportunities
   - Prescribes best practice solutions
   - Applies the scientific problem-solving method

- Selects projects based on achieving the end state
- Focuses improvement on the constraint

IMPACT OF SIR

SIR is created by the capabilities of four methodologies converging to provide a robust process to continuously improve supply chain competitive advantage in alignment with the value proposition of the business. Implementation of SIR is strategic, as market and product strategies will be supported by necessary and sufficient operational performance. No business will maintain a sustainable market leadership position without a continuous improvement strategy and methodology.

REFERENCES

Cohen, Shoshanah, and Joseph Roussel. *Strategic supply chain management.* New York: McGraw Hill, 2005.

Lambert, Doug. *Supply chain management.* Sarasota, FL: Supply Management Institute, 2004.

Lambert, Doug. *Supply chain management.* Sarasota, FL: Supply Management Institute, 2006.

Ohno, Taiichi. *Toyota production system: Beyond large-scale production.* Cambridge MA: Productivity Press, 1988.

Womack, James P., Daniel T. Jones, and Daniel Roos. *The machine that changed the world.* New York: Rawson Associates, 1990.

4

The Role of the CEO: Creating the Vision

A leader's vision defines direction and goals, and sets priorities for the improvements to the supply chain required to create or increase a competitive advantage. Various tools, such as benchmarking, simulation modeling, and value stream mapping are used to construct a current-state view of the supply chain, define goals, and identify the changes. The analytical process is used to answer key supply chain strategic and operational performance questions such as

- What distinct supply chains exist within our business?
- What is each supply chain's competitive reality?
- Is there a supply chain vision to deliver competitive advantage for customers?
- How does current financial and operational performance compare with that of peer companies and competitors in the markets served?
- How do current practices compare with best practices of leading companies and industries?
- What supply chain priority improvements are needed?
- How can organizations be energized and motivated by committing to transformational change?

Step one in applying SIR (Sustainable Improvement Roadmap) is to create a compelling vision that will address these questions.

LEARNED FROM EXPERIENCE: PAUL

**LEADERS GET RESULTS, BUT THEY ARE
ALSO OBLIGATED TO BE BUILDERS**

Twenty-plus years ago, I was a plant manager and my daughter gave me a framed quotation from the old testament, Proverbs 29:18 *Where there is no vision, the people perish.* I have had this on the front of my desk as I moved through nine assignments since then. It reminds me every day that operational performance is a minimum standard, providing a clear vision to which the organization should aspire and by which it should be challenged, and is a leadership obligation. We are fortunate to be given the opportunity to lead; we need to be sure that we are good stewards of what we are given and leave things for the next generation better than we found them.

HOW TO FORMULATE THE VISION: FIRST FACE REALITY, THEN COMMUNICATE IT

In his book *Confronting Reality* (2004), Larry Bossidy states, "The tools, practices, and behaviors that will distinguish success from failure can be summed up in one phrase: relentless realism" (p.12). Frequently leaders with good intentions fail to confront reality because they don't want to take the risk transformational change requires. The process always involves organizational uncertainty, potentially affecting people who have been colleagues for many years. The leader also assumes significant career risk because of the potential for failure or board of director impatience.

Another common reality is avoidance behavior resulting from arrogance brought on by past success. Companies with strong intellectual property or with superior market positions frequently believe "we're different," "we're better," or "that won't happen to us."

Unfortunately avoiding reality leads to the worst outcomes for leaders, companies, and their employees because it opens opportunities for aggressive competitors. Leaders are responsible for keeping organizations grounded in reality, as competitive advantage is temporary and must be continuously built and maintained. Most people want to know exactly where they stand and they respect leaders who keep them grounded in reality. Executives who shield people from reality and its risk also deny them an opportunity to make choices involving their careers, families, and the company. Doing this underestimates people and does not recognize their ability to make right choices.

Organizations are motivated to embrace change when their members are fully informed about the risks to success of their company, and they feel leadership respects them as full partners in company success. Toyota's leadership demonstrated this in 2002 when they asked all plants and suppliers to reduce costs by 30 to 40 percent in three years to counter emerging threats from Korean and Chinese auto manufacturers. By 2004 the Georgetown, Kentucky, engine plant was well on its way toward achieving these goals, a clear demonstration of Toyota's forward thinking and the power of Lean continuous improvement.

LEARNED FROM EXPERIENCE: DAN

LEADERS ARE RESPONSIBLE FOR HOLDING THE REALITY MIRROR UP TO THE ENTIRE COMPANY

Leading a supply chain analysis project at a $1.5-billion company, the cross-functional team identified over $40 million of opportunities across the enterprise. To achieve these savings required significant changes in its organization, processes, and people. Two years later, almost no hard savings had been achieved in spite of a large and well-organized Six Sigma capability. Executive-level motivation did not exist to inflict transformational change on the company as their near-term survival didn't depend on it. Forward-thinking team members saw the elephant in the room, as they had made careful comparisons to key competitors and knew the company was behind in implementing leading management methods and industry best practices. Leaders should never underestimate the intelligence of their team; it will kill credibility.

Sustaining transformational change requires a motivated and committed team that believes its professional and personal success is linked directly to transformation success. Facing reality's threats, risks, and opportunities generates energy to embrace radical change and creates commitment vital to overcoming barriers in a long journey of change. Once an organization is ready to face reality, the conditions are present to begin applying SIR.

THE SUSTAINABLE IMPROVEMENT ROADMAP

SIR uses three tools to define the current operational performance reality and create the information required to gain total team commitment to change.

1. Financial performance comparison to competitive and peer companies in the same market.
2. SCOR (Supply Chain Operations Reference model) benchmarking *vis-à-vis* peer companies in the same market or from best-performing industries.
3. Material and work and information flow analysis using SCOR and Lean current-state versus future-state value stream maps.

Examination of reality starts by establishing a clear picture of current financial and operational performance, and creating knowledge for developing a strategic approach to competing effectively. Since the scope of SCOR assessment is the entire supply chain and all of its processes, SIR starts by applying SCOR, defining individual supply chains within the business.

> **LEARNED FROM EXPERIENCE: DAN AND PAUL**
>
> **MANAGE TO MEET DIFFERENT EXPECTATIONS**
>
> 3M floppy disk manufacturing was an intensely competitive business requiring a sustained unit cost improvement rate of 15 to 20 percent per year for 10 years. While improvement efforts were primarily focused on cost, growth and satisfied customers were also necessary for survival. Entering two new markets, lessons about different market segments' service and quality expectations were learned the hard way. Japan was the first new market. When volume shipments began

to 3M Japan, a high percentage of product was rejected for quality reasons. These were the same floppy disks supplied to U.S. markets, so the organization was stumped about the source of the problem. The difference turned out to be expectations. Eventually we were successful in Japan, but only after we established a formal quality improvement team and addressed issues in monthly teleconferences with our colleagues in Japan.

The second market was the computer OEM (original equipment manufacturers) market. These customers valued quality and delivery performance above cost, but plant processes weren't geared to respond efficiently. They were incredibly demanding about having exactly the right color on packaging materials, meeting their quality expectations, and delivering perfectly.

Both 3M Japan and the OEMs represented different customer groups with different priorities. Success was achieved by managing these supply chains differently to meet their expectations.

This is done by creating a matrix of product families and customer groups (Figure 4.1). Segments of *customer groups* (customers who have similar buying behaviors) have common expectations from suppliers. This provides "voice of the customer" requirements, which in turn enables the supply chain's business processes to align with those requirements. Major product families used by these customer groups identify the specific supply chains that deliver those products through an integrated set of activities.

Once supply chains are defined, a balanced set of supply chain metrics is needed to understand company performance. These metrics must provide a "voice of customer" and an operational view of performance to provide a balanced picture of business health.

CREATING VALUE FOR CUSTOMERS

One consistent theme of Lean, Six Sigma, and SCOR is *customer*. The voice of the customer, their needs, expectations, and priorities, must be satisfied to have sustained business success. Leading businesses tend to

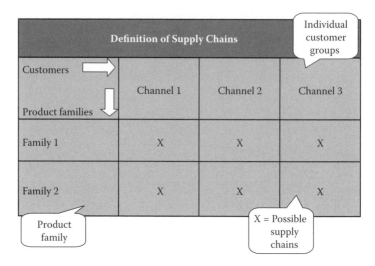

FIGURE 4.1
Supply chains defined.

be best at focusing on customer value–driven metrics and goals, and are frequently in highly competitive markets such as consumer-packaged goods, automotive OEM (original equipment manufacturer), or consumer electronics. Customers in these markets demand very specific performance and failure has direct consequences on suppliers. They insist on face-to-face meetings to discuss performance, give feedback, and ask for a commitment to improve. In these markets, collaboration is a requirement so suppliers clearly understand performance standards of each big customer are clearly understood.

Unfortunately, in many other markets, even where customers are not as demanding, it is rare for companies to have fully aligned supply chain metrics. It is much more common for companies to live with inherently conflicting metrics when it comes to meeting customer expectations. This issue is especially disturbing because companies often believe they have great metrics and customer alignment even when it is not the case. Consider the example of a company/supplier relationship where both parties were measuring "on-time delivery." After a careful comparison of their metrics, they learned that the supplier considered "on-time delivery" to be equivalent to "on-time shipping" because the customer was responsible for transportation. The customer, however, had a more traditional view of on-time delivery. To them it meant "on the dock." With the exception of a few rare companies, who have exceptional supply chain alignment, most operate this way every day.

The tendency for metrics to be conceived and implemented in isolation is widespread. Every place we see the word *manager* in an organization chart, we automatically have a little metrics engine creating, modifying, and changing a vast array of measurements. While it is important that each manager be measured with a set of metrics, it is essential they are well aligned to external or internal customers. Unfortunately, such alignment is rare. The result for most organizations is a vast number of metrics and metric targets loosely aligned at best and frequently in conflict with one another.

Because of the critical importance of customers, it follows that everything done in a business should first be viewed through the customers' eyes. A company's especially important metrics or KPIs (Key Performance Indicators) must have a "line of sight" to customer expectations, which means that the company's metrics are well enough aligned with the customer's to be valid predictors of customer satisfaction and indicators of customer value.

CUSTOMER VALUE

Step one in determining your company's supply chain metrics is to understand how your supply chain impacts customers, and specifically how it impacts a customer's EVA (Economic Value Added). EVA measures the true financial health of an enterprise. It is based on the principle that a company's financial health is measured by how much net profit exceeds the cost of invested capital.

Figure 4.2 illustrates a breakdown of customer EVA. Net profit is derived by subtracting cost of goods sold, general and administrative cost, and taxes from sales. Starting at the net profit box in Figure 4.2, you can view the elements of this calculation. The total cost of invested capital is the result of multiplying the cost of capital by total company assets. EVA is the result of subtracting the total cost of capital from net profit. The SCOR model recognized the need to measure supply chain performance and, therefore, developed a list of cross-industry performance attributes to guide us in selecting KPIs. These are as follows:

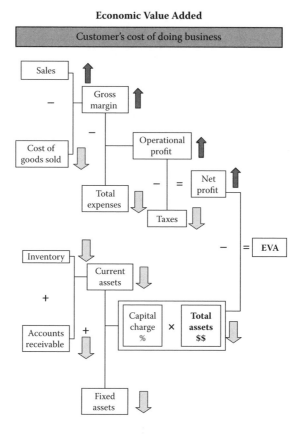

FIGURE 4.2
Economic value added.

1. *Flexibility:* ability to respond to unplanned demand
2. *Cost:* amount spent to supply product or manage the supply chain
3. *Delivery reliability:* dependability in getting the product to the customer on time
4. *Responsiveness:* the amount of time it takes to fill orders; the sooner the better
5. *Asset management:* utilization of fixed and working assets

There is clear alignment between EVA and SCOR performance attributes (Figure 4.3).

For example, a supplier's delivery reliability can have an impact on customers' lost sales, lost customers, and lost sales opportunities. If a

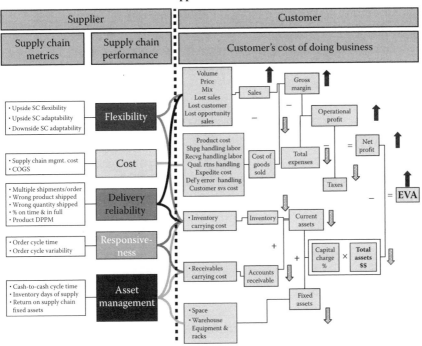

FIGURE 4.3
SCOR–EVA performance attributes.

promised delivery fails to arrive on time, has unacceptable quality, or is late, the customer may not be able to fulfill their customers' orders. Poor delivery performance also affects inventory levels. Unreliable delivery causes customers to compensate by carrying extra inventory. A similar comparison can be made among the other four performance attributes and EVA drivers.

In addition to connecting EVA to SCOR, these performance attributes are designed to ensure a balanced set of supply chain metrics (measuring all important supply chain aspects, but no more) is developed. Using SCOR performance attributes as a guide, at least one metric per category is established. It is not unlike an automobile dashboard that has many gauges and lights but is missing an oil pressure indicator—everything seems to be running fine until low oil pressure results in engine failure. Similarly, metrics or KPIs need balance to ensure that all-important areas of performance are in focus. Once specific drivers of customer value are understood, metrics aligned to those drivers and their required performance standards can be defined and validated by customers.

Using SCOR's five Level 1 performance attributes as a guide, we should seek to establish at least one metric per category for starters. Recommended SCOR model metrics are shown in Figure 4.4; however, these are not the only possible metrics for each category. For example, in the category of delivery reliability, typical choices might include the following:

- On-time delivery
- On-time shipping
- Fill-rate
- Perfect order fulfillment (SCOR)

A useful guideline when identifying metrics is to set aside constraints and seek to define the best metric possible, one that will measure customer expectation most precisely. Once this ideal metric is defined, data collection methods must be considered. Measurement constraints are likely to appear and it might be necessary to compromise. For example, for a metric such as on-time delivery, actual delivery times may not be available, so initially it may be necessary to measure on-time shipping.

SCOR Level 1 Metrics

	Attribute	Metric (level 1)
Customer	Reliability	Perfect order fulfillment
Customer	Responsiveness	Order fulfillment cycle time
Customer	Agility (flexibility)	Supply-chain flexibility
Customer	Agility (flexibility)	Supply-chain adaptability
Internal	Cost	Supply-chain management cost
Internal	Cost	Cost of goods sold
Internal	Assets	Cash-to-cash cycle time
Internal	Assets	Return on supply chain fixed assets

FIGURE 4.4
SCOR Level 1 metrics.

FINANCIAL AND OPERATIONAL BENCHMARKING

Once supply chain metrics are identified, benchmarking can proceed. Financial benchmarking of publicly traded competitors and market peers is most commonly done using their 10-K reports, which are available from various benchmark services such as Hoovers and Forbes. Data of privately held competitors is not reported publicly and, therefore, not included in available data sources. Data is also available from free sources but only at the company level, so comparison to multidivision competitors is not possible. The company's chief financial officer (CFO) can provide these benchmark comparisons from available sources.

Financial benchmarking builds a business case by gaining insight into supply chain improvement opportunities. Operational benchmarking data gathering may require multiple sources to get a comprehensive picture. APQC (American Productivity and Quality Council), a free service for Supply Chain Council members, is an excellent source of benchmarking data. APQC provides industry-level data but has limited capability to provide data below industry level. Other data sources include trade associations, published articles and reports, benchmarking services, and customers. Customers normally evaluate suppliers using common criteria. They compare market peers to standards established by the best suppliers' performances; therefore, not having direct competitors in a benchmarking process doesn't diminish its value, because the goal is satisfying customers.

CASE STUDY: TWIN CITY MANUFACTURING

Twin City Manufacturing is a fictitious company, but its story is based on the authors' actual experiences. We will tell it in the remaining chapters to illustrate key principles, tools, and examples to guide you through the implementation process.

Step 1: Assess the Current State of the Business

Twin City Manufacturing (TCM) is an original equipment manufacturer (OEM) supplier of specialized metal components. These specialized stamped and powdered-formed metal components are designed with unique thermal and conductive properties. The standardized components are assembled into modular designed finished products, which are defined by customer specifications.

Twin City is the largest of four specialized metal components suppliers and has a 100-year history of product innovation and quality. Three competitors entered the market in the past two decades. The past 10 years have been particularly difficult for Twin City as sales increased at a slower rate than market growth, and two competitors consistently grew faster than TCM. Twin City continues to have product innovation leadership, but top competitors have quickly learned to follow with alternative solutions that don't conflict with Twin City's intellectual property.

Company leadership has been rationalizing their situation until recently when a new CEO, Rick Hamilton, was appointed from outside TCM. He was selected by the board because of his strong operations background in manufacturing, logistics, and planning. He is a Six Sigma Black Belt, TOC-certified Jonah (a certification received from the Goldratt Institute), and Lean manufacturing expert (as a plant manager of a supplier to Toyota), and he used SCOR in his last assignment as operations vice president of the same automotive OEM supplier. Rick spent his first 30 days getting to know TCM operations and team members. He was impressed by everyone's intense loyalty to Twin City Manufacturing and liked what he saw in his leadership team and the competences of functional organizations.

1. COO (Chief Operating Officer) Eaton Oesterlein was a prototypical operations executive with a single-minded focus on meeting his operating plan. He possessed strong persuasion skills with a direct communications style and was respected by everyone in the company. Fred Gilligan, CFO, was unusual in that he was very engaged in business strategy, spent significant time coaching all levels of the organization on business finance, and openly shared financial information inside TCM. He could be tough when necessary, but always tempered his criticism with constructive coaching. Odair Brazil, an extremely strong sales executive, had career-long relationships with key customers, allowing him to maintain business with customers in spite of their complaints about TCM quality and service. Human Resources Manager Charlie Dubey had a good reputation with all

organizational levels and championed development of all employees. Susan Zoelzer, the engineering manager, was a very strong technical and project manager possessing personal traits commonly found in great engineers; she listened more than she talked, spoke her mind, and was intolerant of people not keeping their promises. Rick had reached some conclusions about TCM: It was losing market share and profitability at an accelerating pace.

2. There was no clear strategy aligning customer value and all aspects of company operations.

3. Each function operated independently to achieve its goals.

4. The executive team seemed to get along well, but they lived in an environment best described as cordial anarchy, where they treated one another respectfully, but everyone did his or her own thing; true teamwork didn't exist.

5. The company had a long history of technical excellence and innovation.

6. The company needed significant change to regain market share and improve declining profitability.

With his assessment, he turned his attention to working with his team to better understand the company's supply chain, and operational and financial performance. Twin City Manufacturing's supply chain was simple. Their specialized metal components, which they sold to companies in the medical field, accounted for 95 percent of sales (Figure 4.5).

Twin City Manufacturing Supply Chains			
Customers ⟹ Product families ⬇	Medical applications	Sports applications	High-tech applications
Metal components	95% of revenue	2% of revenue	3% of revenue

FIGURE 4.5
Twin City Manufacturing's supply chains.

Step 2: Assess the Supply Chain Using SCOR Benchmarking

Rick asked Fred Gilligan (CFO) and Eaton Oesterlein (COO) to complete the SCOR benchmark assessment. In order to understand the project's scope, they built a high-level map of their medical supply chain and identified its configuration using SCOR supply chain configuration nomenclature (i.e., M2 = make-to-order, S2 = source make-to-order items, D2 = deliver make-to-order items). A supply chain map is a good level-setting process, which ensures that teams start with a clear understanding of the project's scope.

Fred Gilligan led the exercise, mapping TCM's current supply chain including key suppliers, key customers, and company operations. Product from Twin City is shipped to OEM customers who assemble them into their final products (Figure 4.6). Fred and Eaton completed benchmarking data collection of 20 measurements (Figure 4.7). Fred located data from financial reporting sources and industry associations, constructing a good picture of key peer suppliers and competitors. Eaton used their customers' top supplier performance feedback data to complete benchmarking

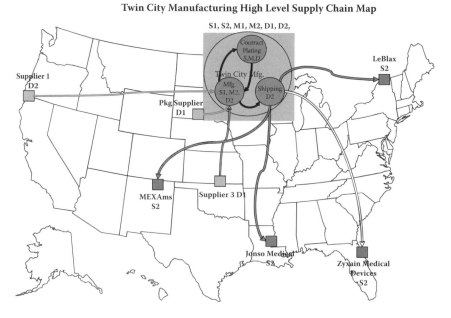

Twin City Manufacturing High Level Supply Chain Map

FIGURE 4.6

Twin City Manufacturing's supply chain map. SMD = Source, make, deliver. SI = SCOR source process level 1. DI = SCOR deliver process level 1.

Twin City Manufacturing Benchmark Data

Performance Category	Delivery Performance %	Line Fill Rate %	Perfect Order Fulfillment	Order Fulfillment L.T.	Production Flexibility	Cost of Goods Sold %	Total Supply Chain Cost %	SGA Cost %	Cost % Warranty/Returns	Cash-to-Cash Cycle in Days	Days of Inventory	Asset Turns	Gross Margin	Operating Income %	Net Income %	Value Added per Employee ($000)	Return on Assets	3 yr CAGR %	Revenue ($000,000)	Number of Employees
Twin City Manufacturing	85%	87%	39%	17	40	70%	13%	21%	6%	75	55	3.5	30.0%	9.0%	6.1%	$21	8.3%	4%	$260	775
Company A	83%	85%	25%	15	35	75%	11%	18%	9%	80	64	4.0	25%	7%	4.8%	$13	7.5%	0%	$140	500
Company B	86%	86%	40%	10	38	73%	13%	18%	9%	70	60	4.7	27%	9%	6.1%	$20	9.2%	4%	$125	375
Company C	89%	91%	50%	12	30	73%	10%	16%	8%	64	54	5.0	27%	11%	7.5%	$23	10.2%	4%	$450	1475
Company D	90%	92%	70%	8	20	72%	9%	16%	5%	65	51	5.5	28%	12%	8.2%	$30	11.5%	6%	$160	430
Company E	92%	93%	45%	11	25	72%	8%	17%	6%	65	40	6.0	28%	11%	7.5%	$22	13.0%	5%	$320	1100
Company F	96%	98%	85%	6	10	68%	6%	14%	4%	55	35	7.0	32%	18%	12.2%	$42	19.0%	8%	$285	825
Company G	78%	81%	27%	14	45	78%	13%	20%	10%	90	74	2.0	22%	2%	1.4%	$5	2.4%	-3%	$700	2100
Company H	91%	94%	65%	9	15	71%	7%	15%	5%	50	40	4.7	29%	14%	9.5%	$26	12.0%	7%	$210	760
Company I	87%	88%	60%	11	35	75%	12%	18%	8%	80	65	3.0	25%	7%	4.8%	$14	6.0%	2%	$460	1600
Company J	82%	81%	50%	13	45	79%	14%	19%	12%	87	72	2.1	21%	2%	1.4%	$21	2.0%	-2%	$175	115
Median	87.0%	88.0%	50.0%	11.0	35.0	73.0%	11.0%	18.0%	8.0%	70	55.0	4.7	27.0%	9.0%	6.1%	$21	9.2%	4.0%	$260	775
Advantage	91.4%	93.3%	62.5%	9.5	22.5	71.5%	8.5%	16.0%	5.5%	65	45.5	5.3	28.5%	11.5%	7.8%	$25	11.8%	5.5%	$385	1288
Best in Class	94.8%	96.5%	70.0%	8.0	15.0	70.0%	7.0%	15.0%	5.0%	55	40.0	6.0	30.0%	14.0%	9.5%	$30	13.0%	7.0%	$460	1600

FIGURE 4.7

SCOR benchmark data. L.T. = Lead Time. SGA = Sales, General, and Administrative expenses. CAGR = Compound Annual Growth Rate.

information. This data included all their top competitors and peer companies with company names coded as suppliers A, B, C, etc. Based on experience, he sorted out the coded data and determined operational service performance of their three top competitors and key peer companies. Fred analyzed and organized the information and prepared a chart for their first review meeting (Figure 4.7).

SCOR Benchmarking Results

Fred gave a copy of the benchmark data to each team member. The Twin City results were color coded—black is less than median, grey is at median, and white is at advantage or best in class; unfortunately, black dominated the page. TCM's management team was stunned; they questioned the validity of the data, complained that Fred was always presenting everything in the most negative light, and finally agreed among themselves that last year was just a bad year. Fred responded that a review of the previous year's data resulted in an identical outcome. The group continued to grumble among themselves, but had no choice but to accept brutal reality; Twin City's performance was median or less across a majority of measured parameters.

Rick Hamilton discussed the results with his team, eventually convincing them of the tremendous opportunity this data represented. They could once again become market leaders. He also challenged them to take ownership of "this once-in-a-career opportunity" to lead a transformational change. They had an opportunity to establish their own mark and legacy at Twin City Manufacturing. Eventually, after getting over their shock, defensiveness, and anger from internalizing harsh reality, they moved on to discussing next steps.

Step 3: Review Strategy

The Twin City Manufacturing executive team had added a number of new members in the last year. Before gathering, the voice of customer information, Rich Hamilton, decided to have Odair (sales and marketing executive vice president) conduct a marketing executive review explaining the company's approach to strategy and their current strategies. Odair started the discussion with a review of strategy development concepts used by the company.

Twin City's strategic approach was based on Michael Treacy and Fred Wiersema's book *The Discipline of Market Leaders* (1995), which is a practical approach to developing a business strategy. The purpose of business is to create value for investors, and strategy defines a superior value proposition intended to create economic value growth faster than competitors do. Treacy and Wiersema define three core strategy choices: (1) operational excellence, (2) product leadership, and (3) customer intimacy; and they define four rules necessary for success regardless of the overall strategy selected:

1. Provide the best market offering by excelling in a specific dimension of value.
2. Maintain threshold standards on other dimensions of value.
3. Dominate your market by improving value year after year.
4. Build a well-tuned operating model dedicated to delivering unmatched value.

These four rules are a powerful affirmation of supply chain importance to successful business strategy. In his book, *What Is Strategy?* Michael Porter (1996) defined *operating models* as a "different set of activities or activities done in a different way to create a unique mix of value" (p. 62).

The strategies of TCM's competitors were evident in analyzing their data. Competitor F chose operational excellence as their core strategy, building an operational model to provide a superior level of delivery performance very efficiently. Benchmark results (Figure 4.7) validated their strategy as they had superior performance in delivery reliability. Competitor H chose customer intimacy as its core strategy and built an operating model with superior responsiveness and flexibility, which was also confirmed by benchmarking results.

TCM understood why they had been losing market share. Their top two competitors had chosen unique strategies, supported by well-designed operating models ensuring effective operational implementation. TCM had become complacent and had not recognized that performance gaps had evolved over time, resulting in their current weakened competitive position (Figure 4.8). Twin City Manufacturing maintained market leadership for decades through a *product leadership strategy*, that is, by providing innovative products that delivered differentiated value.

Increasingly competitive markets valued their innovation, but in recent years the demand for operational excellence in delivery and responsiveness had grown. Twin City Manufacturing did not need to

Supply Chain Operations Alignment with Business Strategy

Supply Chain Performance Attributes		Business Strategy		
		Competitor F	TCM	Competitor H
		Operational Excellence	Product Leadership	Customer Intimacy
Customer Facing	Delivery reliability	Superior	Disadvantage	Advantage
	Responsiveness	Advantage	Median	Superior
	Flexibility	Advantage	Disadvantage	Superior
Internally Facing	Cost	Superior	Advantage	Advantage
	Asset management	Superior	Disadvantage	Median

FIGURE 4.8
Benchmarking Twin City Manufacturing supply chain operation.

change its fundamental strategy, but it did need to achieve superior supply chain performance in those supply chain attributes that were linked to their distinct product innovation competence. For the remaining supply chain performance attributes, those that most closely supported an operational excellence strategy, they needed to achieve at least threshold performance.

TCM had learned the hard way that not meeting at least minimum threshold performance or market parity had resulted in the loss of their market-leading position. This strategic assessment of their supply chain defined the challenge they faced in eliminating competitive disadvantage and restoring credibility and value to their product leadership strategy. TCM executives could see they had lost touch with key customers and needed to reverse this situation quickly—it was a crisis. Rick asked every team member to visit key customers, validate their benchmark results, and understand customers' perspectives on TCM's loss of market share and slow growth. He taught sales executive Odair the customer economic value added methodology and asked him to lead their team in visiting key customers, documenting their expectations and priorities.

LEARNED FROM EXPERIENCE: PAUL

At 3M Brazil in 1997, we realized our supply chains were not capable of meeting the needs of key market segments, and in fact, we had used generic metrics, which had no meaning to the customer, for measuring our internal performance. We started a very ambitious program by assigning a full-time team to redesign our business processes.

The project turned out to be much bigger than we had anticipated as we discovered how many of our commercial business practices affected supply chains. For example, pricing and merchandising practices were impacting supply chain performance and needed to be included in the reengineering. As a result, nearly two years were spent reengineering processes before we could begin enterprise resource planning (ERP) system implementation in 1999.

ERP system modifications were made to institutionalize our new business practices. For example, when it came to inventory allocation, we wanted to make sure every part of our operational model "treated our best customers better," so we modified the allocation process to ensure that orders from our "A" classified customers received the first allocation of inventory. In addition, we placed codes on shipping boxes identifying these customers. Transportation companies were trained so that when capacity limitations required a decision about priority, they had the information to make the right choice for 3M preferred customers. From 1995 to 2000 we significantly outgrew the markets we served and our operating margins increased 30 percent.

CREATING VALUE FOR CUSTOMERS

Odair Brazil walked the leadership team through the process for defining customer value. He was enthusiastic about having Rick and his employees in the field gathering customer value information. The success of any strategy requires superior satisfaction with target customers. Understanding customer needs, expectations, and priorities requires a depth of information that can only be obtained through continuous relationships, and it is not possible for a business to have a deep collaborative relationship with all of its customers. Identifying a segment of customers who want to have collaborative supplier relationships answers this apparent dilemma. Building a deep understanding of this selected set of customers provides information needed to ensure business strategy is aligned with customers' real needs and priorities.

Step 4: Gather Customer Information

A plan was needed for efficiently gathering customer information, but first, key questions required answers:

1. What information is needed?
2. Which customers shall we approach?
3. What process will we use?

After much discussion, they defined four key pieces of customer information that they needed to understand:

1. the customer's business priorities;
2. the customer's view of TCM's performance, including data if available;
3. the customer's assessment of how TCM ranked against the competition; and
4. specific issues the customer had with TCM.

Data desired from each selected customer included the following:

1. Customer's measurement of TCM's on-time delivery
2. Customer's measurement of TCM's delivered quality
3. Customer's measurement of TCM's perfect order fulfillment
4. Customer's experience with TCM's order fulfillment lead time

TCM knew that it would be impossible to approach all of its customers. Odair had created a customer list from largest to smallest based on sales and selected three large customers that were critically important to TCM's business. Next, the team reviewed the remaining list of customers, searching for other strategically important customers. Results from this search added one company, for a total of four candidates from which TCM could gain an understanding of in-depth customer needs and priorities; these four companies were to be visited.

Using an EVA chart and five SCOR performance attributes (Figure 4.3), they developed several questions to pose to the four key customers.

1. Of these five performance attributes, which is your top priority and which is your second?
2. How does TCM rank against similar suppliers in each of these five customer measures?
   - On-time delivery
   - Delivered quality
   - Other delivery issues
   - Perfect order fulfillment
   - Order fulfillment lead time
3. For each performance category, what performance level is required to be your best supplier?

TCM executives visited customers and learned that they continued to value Twin City's innovation and new products, but service on established products was not acceptable and was hurting the customers' business. In addition, competitors had shorter order fulfillment cycle times allowing customers to carry lower inventory (Figure 4.9).

The bottom line was that Twin City's product leadership strategy had become ineffective due to poor service, resulting in the loss of business gained through introduction of new products to competitors who offered better service. Their best competitors followed fast with new products, which were displacing TCM's new products despite having poorer performance. Benchmark results were validated by customer feedback, making it clear that TCM's operational system needed to be redesigned to consistently meet the delivery reliability, quality, and responsiveness expectations of their customers.

Customer Priorities

TCM Actual Performance	1st Priority	2nd Priority	On-time Delivery	Delivered Quality	Other Delivery Issues	Perfect Order Fulfillment	Order Fulfillment Cycle Time
LeBlax	Delivery reliability	Responsiveness	62%	77.4%	85%	40.8%	19 Days
MexAms	Responsiveness	Delivery reliability	59%	70.3%	87%	36.1%	16 Days
Jonso Medical	Delivery reliability	Responsiveness	64%	74%	84%	39.8%	17 Days
Zyxain Medical	Delivery reliability	Responsiveness	60%	79.2%	86%	40.9%	16 Days
Overall	Delivery reliability	Responsiveness	61.3%	75.2%	85.5%	39.4%	17.0 Days

Best Performance			On-time Delivery	Delivered Quality	Other Delivery Issues	Perfect Order Fulfillment	Order Fulfillment Cycle Time
LeBlax			88%	88%	99%	85%	9 Days
MexAms			92%	95%	97%	65%	8 Days
Jonso Medical			95%	93%	95%	70%	7 Days
Zyxain Medical			91%	97%	95%	55%	9 Days
Benchmarks			91.5%	93.3%	96.5%	69%	8.25

FIGURE 4.9
Assessing customer priorities.

LEARNED FROM EXPERIENCE: DAN

THERE IS GREAT POWER IN A CROSS-FUNCTIONAL TEAM MAPPING THE SUPPLY CHAIN TO BETTER UNDERSTAND THE BUSINESS AND THE INTERCONNECTEDNESS OF ITS FUNCTIONAL SILOS

At one company, our SCOR supply chain analysis revealed it had been growing at a 10 percent annual rate primarily through acquisition of smaller but similar companies. However, there was little integration of these companies, which continued operating with much of their original structure, processes, general manager, P&L (profit and loss), and even sales organizations intact. We identified eight individual supply chains in this quagmire of operations. Interestingly, they crossed organizational lines, and by documenting performance, we learned one of them was actually unprofitable, a fact that was previously indiscernible using their existing P&L structure.

The executive team discussed their Sustainable Improvement Roadmap plan scorecard for their strategic plan and decided to use a mix of seven SCOR Level 1 metrics (Figure 4.10).

Benchmark results are presented in five columns, which divide benchmark data populations into these categories:

- Column 1: Bottom quartile of performance—a major opportunity.
- Column 2: Second quartile of performance—a competitive disadvantage.
- Column 3: Average or median performance.
- Column 4: Seventy-fifth percentile of performance—a competitive advantage.
- Column 5: Ninetieth percentile of performance—a superior position versus competition.

Twin City Manufacturing benchmark results (Figure 4.10) defined performance gaps from current levels to median, advantage, and superior performance. Two columns on the far right quantify potential benefits of achieving these performance levels, building a business case for change. TCM executives realized this assessment provided a clear picture of current performance and gaps, which could be prioritized to align with their business strategy and customer priorities. They realized that this information would mobilize their organization once they communicated

Twin City Manufacturing SCOR Benchmark Summary

Key Perspectives / Metrics L1 = SCOR Level 1 Metric		Major Oppor-tunity	Disadvantage	Average or Median	Advantage	Superior	◆ To Advantage	△ Addn'l to Superior
Delivery Performance/ Quality	Delivery performance to request L1		■		◆	△	3% + 3% One time sales Incr.	2% + 2% Annual sales Incr.
	Perfect order fulfillment L1		■		◆	△	23% pts.	8% pts.
Flexibility & Responsiveness	Upside production flexibility L1		■		◆	△	Required to improve delivery performance to request	
	Order fulfillment lead time (MTO) L1	■			◆	△	–7.5 Days	–2 Days
Cost	Supply-chain management cost L1	■			◆	△	$11.70 M/yr	$3.9 M/yr
Working Capital	Cash-to-cash cycle time L1		■		◆	△	10 Day reduction	10 Day reduction
	Net asset turns L1		■		◆	△	1.8 Turns $25.3 M Inv.	0.7 Turns $6.0 M Inv.
Total Benefit Included in S.C. Management cost*		First full year operating profit benefit					$16.3 M	$6.0 M
		One time inventory reduction					$25.3 M	$6.0 M

Supply-Chain Performance Versus Custom Population

■ TCM position

FIGURE 4.10
Twin City Manufacturing SCOR benchmark summary.

these results broadly across TCM. They were confident their entire team would be engaged, be challenged, and respond positively, as everyone at Twin City wanted to be part of a winning team and contribute to regaining market leadership.

Step 5: Make the Business Case

Twin City revised its strategic plan including improving supply chain performance to regain competitiveness. They realized that market leadership could be reestablished and sustained using this assessment methodology to guide the journey. They also understood that competitive benchmark performance is not static because their competitors are always improving, and therefore achievement of advantage position might not be enough if competitors are improving at a similar or higher pace. This meant that some level of competitive benchmarking needed to be done each year as a part of strategic planning. Next, one-year goals (Figure 4.11) were set to progress toward closing identified supply-chain performance gaps, which would be required to reestablish market leadership.

Twin City's executives spent two days together reviewing results and determining their path forward. Transformational change was required and would be an enormous task that would take two to three years. After two long days of debate, they agreed on the following assumptions and goals:

1. Twin City Manufacturing commits to growing faster than market average in one year with
   - superior delivery performance to request and perfect order fulfillment performance and
   - advantage performance in upside production flexibility and supply-chain response time.
2. Once these targets are achieved, efforts will be redirected toward improving performance in other year-one plan metrics.
3. Until service goals are achieved, cost and working capital goals will be secondary. One-year cost goals are to reach parity performance and working capital performance, as this should be a consequence of optimizing order fulfillment cycle time.
4. Twin City Manufacturing is committed to pooling all existing improvement resources and generating additional project resources as a result of early improvement because resources can't be added due to current financial performance.

Twin City Manufacturing SIR Year-One Goals

Key Perspectives	SCOR Level 1 Metrics	Supply-Chain Performance Versus Custom Population						☆ 1 yr. Plan
		Major Opportunity	Disadvantage	Average or Median	Advantage	Superior		
Delivery Performance/ Quality	Delivery performance to request	■		◆		☆		5% + 5% $3.9 M/yr + $3.9 M yr
	Perfect order fulfillment	■		◆		☆		+ 31% pts
Flexibility & Responsiveness	Upside production flexibility	■			☆		△	Required capability
	Order fulfillment lead time (MTO)	■			☆		△	−7.5 Days
Cost	Supply-chain management cost	■		☆	◆		△	−2.0% $5.2 M/yr
Working Capital	Cash-to-cash cycle time	■			☆		△	10 Day reduction
	Net asset turns	■		☆	◆		△	1.2 Turns $19.3 M Inv reduction
Total Benefit Included in S.C. Management cost*		First full year operating profit benefit						$13.0 M
		One time inventory reduction						$19.3 M

■ TCM position   ◆ Advantage   △ Superior

FIGURE 4.11
Twin City Manufacturing's one-year goals.

Achieving Twin City's vision would mean regaining market leadership, satisfying their customers, and dramatically improving operational performance. Fred Gilligan and Eaton Oesterlein quantified the financial benefit of achieving the year-one plan goals.

1. Operating Profit in the first full year would improve by $13.0M through
   - improvement of 2 percent in cost of goods sold;
   - $3.9M incremental operating profit gain from a 5 percent one-time increase in sales as a result of regaining lost customers and stopping erosion of new product sales gains; and
   - $3.9M incremental operating profit gain from a 5 percent increase in annual sales growth.
2. Improving asset turns by 1.2 turns to market parity will result in a $19.3 million one-time cash benefit.

The business case is complete and they have aligned their high-level scorecard financial benefits to each internal operational metric ensuring alignment of internal operations and creating value for their customers.

The final step in constructing a vision was to determine which improvement projects should be given priority and implemented.

Step 6: Build Implementation Plan for Priority Improvements

With their business case complete, attention was turned to defining what needed to be done. Now more homework was needed to understand which processes and practices needed improvement to achieve their goals. Based on customer priorities, the initial focus was on order delivery to request promise date and order fulfillment lead time. They reviewed the SCOR process model to understand which processes were root causes performance gap.

Next, team members decomposed perfect order fulfillment Level 1 metrics (Figure 4.12) down to Level 3, identifying the underperforming processes. The analysis showed multiple process failure areas, including order entry, schedule attainment, packaging quality, product quality, and delivery to commitment—all of which provided major opportunities for improvement and inclusion as implementation plan projects.

The final assessment step was decomposition of order fulfillment lead time. Level 3 analyses (Figure 4.13) identified the processes most likely to be causing current long cycle times and needing further examination. The top suspects were cycle times to schedule, issue materials, build, transfer

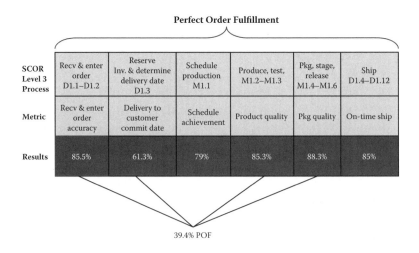

Perfect Order Fulfillment

SCOR Level 3 Process	Recv & enter order D1.1–D1.2	Reserve Inv. & determine delivery date D1.3	Schedule production M1.1	Produce, test, M1.2–M1.3	Pkg, stage, release M1.4–M1.6	Ship D1.4–D1.12
Metric	Recv & enter order accuracy	Delivery to customer commit date	Schedule achievement	Product quality	Pkg quality	On-time ship
Results	85.5%	61.3%	79%	85.3%	88.3%	85%

39.4% POF

FIGURE 4.12
Perfect order fulfillment.

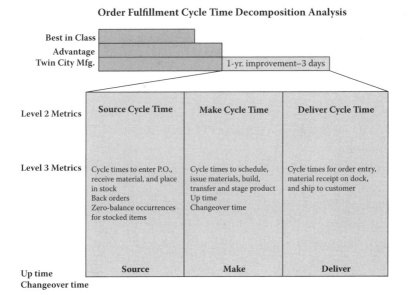

FIGURE 4.13
Order fulfillment cycle time.

and stage the product for shipment as well as order entry cycle times, material receipt on the dock, and shipment to customers.

They reviewed supplier performance using their high-level supply chain map (Figure 4.14) to identify opportunities based on process failures as measured by perfect order fulfillment and order fulfillment lead time decomposition analyses, and concluded the following:

1. Supplier 1 is supplying a make-to-order item. This lengthens their lead time. The supplier has long lead times, poor quality, and poor delivery performance. All these factors may be affecting the delivery performance or order fulfillment cycle time of Twin City Manufacturing.

2. Twin City Manufacturing has long make cycle times and marginal product quality.

3. The delivery performance to request date appears to be caused by failures in schedule attainment and on-time delivery. These failures could result from internal handling delays, carrier performance problems, or problems at customer sites due to delays in receiving product.

Twin City Manufacturing High Level Supply Chain Map

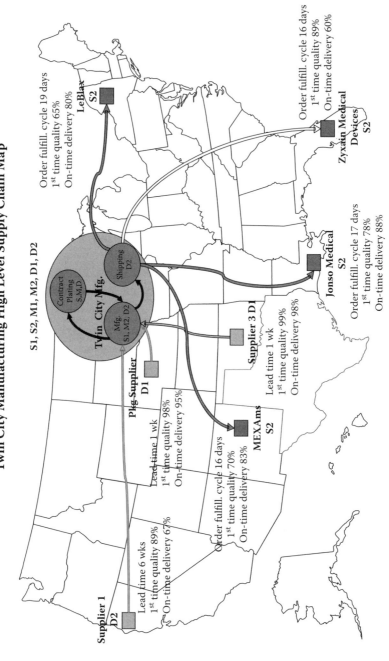

LeBlax
S2

Order fulfill. cycle 19 days
1st time quality 65%
On-time delivery 80%

Zyxain Medical
Devices
S2

Order fulfill. cycle 16 days
1st time quality 89%
On-time delivery 60%

S1, S2, M1, M2, D1, D2

Contract
Plating
S,M,D

Shipping
D2

Twin City Mfg.

Mfg.
S1, M2, D2

Jonso Medical
S2

Order fulfill. cycle 17 days
1st time quality 78%
On-time delivery 88%

Supplier 3 D1

Lead time 1 wk
1st time quality 99%
On-time delivery 98%

Plg Supplier
D1

Lead time 1 wk
1st time quality 98%
On-time delivery 95%

MEXAms
S2

Order fulfill. cycle 16 days
1st time quality 70%
On-time delivery 83%

Supplier 1
D2

Lead time 6 wks
1st time quality 89%
On-time delivery 67%

FIGURE 4.14

Twin City Manufacturing's high-level supply chain map with key supply chain performance data.

Suspected processes were identified, but further analysis was needed to get to root causes and corrective actions. This was a natural time for Rick to introduce value stream mapping—an efficient tool for detailed examination of current processes and practices and identifying root causes that need to be resolved to eliminate these problems.

Rick Hamilton proposed completion of current-state value stream maps, and his team committed to completing their value stream current-state and future-state maps and defining improvements during the following week. The following Monday they met to document their value stream current state beginning with shipping, continuing upstream through all processes, and ending with receiving operations. Rick gave basic instructions regarding what to look for and record, and trained his team using *Learning to See* (1999) by John Shook and Mike Rother, a valuable training book for value stream mapping. They were instructed to do the following (Figure 4.15):

1. Record only important information for each operational process and observe operators to understand how much of their time is truly spent on value-added activity.
    - Performance cycle time, yields, up time, change-over time, etc.
    - Characteristics—number of operators, number of shifts scheduled
2. Document inventory with a triangle indicating days of inventory.
3. Identify types of material flow.
    - Material flow that is pushed to the next process is represented with a solid line.
    - First in, first out (FIFO) flow is a striped line.
    - Material flow that is pulled is represented by dashes and a Kanban card icon.
4. Document in detail the information flow for both internal operations and suppliers using arrows identifying flow direction. Electronic flow is indicated by a "lightning" line.
5. Document total lead time using a step line is created at the bottom of the chart. Days of inventory are noted on the line's top steps and value-added processes are represented on the lower steps. A summary box in the bottom right corner shows total lead time in days and total value-added processing time. The ratio of value-added processing time to total lead-time is an important measure of *Leanness*.

With those brief instructions, they started at shipping, the operation closest to their customers. Shipping operations were originally in a manufacturing building and separate from current plant operations. Material has to be transferred each day to shipping where complete customer orders are assembled. The Shipping Department takes an average of six days to assemble and ship complete customer orders. (Figure 4.15, see 1), Customer delivery time is three days, for a total of nine days of total order fulfillment lead time.

After completing their observations about shipping, the team walked upstream to packaging where the products are packed in bags, boxes, blister packs, and special packages of kits. All operations have throughput rates high enough to be able to handle volumes 50 percent above the current average shipping volume of one million units per day. Packaging machines had low runtimes and scheduling methods did not level flow, causing operator idle time (Figure 4.15, see 2). After recording key packaging operations information, they moved upstream to assembly. Assembly operations contained 15 machines capable of changing over to produce any item in the product line. Current output on three shifts is sufficient to meet the average daily demand. Assembly is scheduled each day based on a review of orders to be shipped and materials in packaging and shipping areas. Day-shift team leaders provide production control with daily schedule recommendations after visual reviews of these areas. At the time, the average inventory on hand in assembly and packaging combined was eight days. These eight days contributed significantly to an order fulfillment lead time of seventeen days (three days shipping time plus six days of inventory in shipping and eight days of inventory between assembly and packaging), which put Twin City at a serious competitive disadvantage.

This push scheduling system is not well synchronized with daily customer demand and is responsible for much of the inventory pile-ups (Figure 4.15, see 3) represented by the triangles before and after assembly.

The team completed key assembly inventory and operational information and then moved upstream to plating and coating operations, which were located in a separate building due to significant environmental and personal protection requirements. Coating and plating, which are not scheduled, have a three-day cycle time and flow material to assembly on a first in, first out (FIFO) basis; 15 days of finished parts inventory wait ahead of assembly operations.

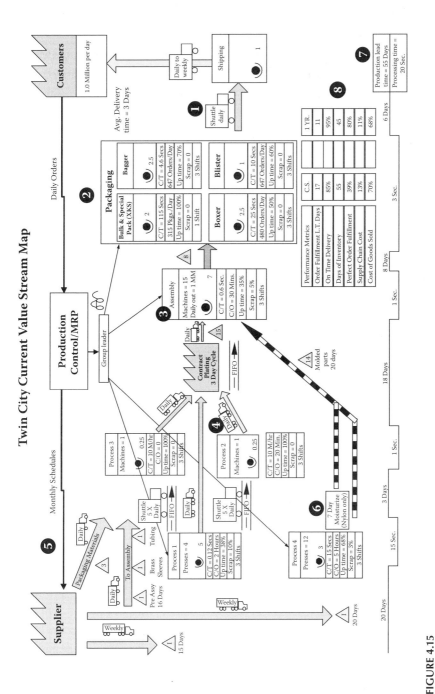

FIGURE 4.15
Twin City Manufacturing's current state value stream map.

The mapping process continued, moving upstream through metal stamping processes 2, 3, and slit-to-width process 1 (Figure 4.15, 4). Operations 2 and 3 are not scheduled because material from operation 1 flows through on a FIFO basis. Operation 1 is scheduled based on Material Requirements Planning (MRP) system priorities, causing inventories to pile up in all downstream operations because it is unable to stay synchronized with daily changes in product mix and volume.

The next location tackled was the raw materials warehouse. Two key suppliers provide 80 percent of its raw material value, so the team focused on materials from these suppliers. Both provide weekly shipments, which suggested that 15 and 20 days of current inventory could be significantly reduced. Inventory of all key raw materials, process information, and scheduling information flow for all operations were noted (Figure 4.15, 5).

The final operation reviewed was insulator molding. This operation had a cycle time of seven days, which restricted the flexibility necessary to run the assembly product mix desired. Key process information was collected and it was noted that cycle time needed to be reduced to one day so that molding could be synchronized with assembly (Figure 4.15, 6).

Completing their current state, they determined the value stream's total value-added process time and total lead time, which are summarized in the bottom right-hand corner of the current-state map (Figure 4.15, 7).

The total production lead time was 55 days, as noted on the benchmarking summary (Figure 4.7), while actual value-added processing time was just 20 seconds. The SIR scorecard performance was added to provide a complete picture (Figure 4.15, 8). The executives were shocked by what they learned through this direct observation approach. Many of their assumptions about how things worked proved false based on recording shop floor reality.

The information was summarized along with their team's observations and opportunities for improvement. Eight areas needing immediate improvement were identified and noted on the current-state value stream map with a grey color burst (Figure 4.16).

For immediate improvement included the following:

1. Increase shuttle frequency to shipping operations to once every hour and schedule two shifts, thus reducing the cycle time of second-shift assembled orders by one day (grey burst 1, Figure 4.16). Increased frequency and shorter cycle times through packaging (see project 2) will

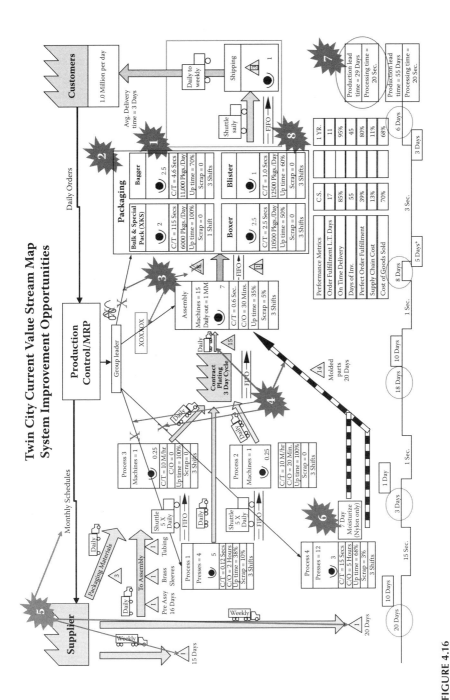

FIGURE 4.16

Twin City Manufacturing's current value stream map illustrating system improvement opportunities.

reduce shipping area inventory from six days to three, which in turn will reduce the order fulfillment lead time by the same three days.

2. Optimize packaging operation (Figure 4.16, grey burst 2).

- Eliminate time wasted by operators replenishing their own packaging materials by setting up a central supermarket (planned inventory of purchased materials) for all packaging items in the warehouse and having materials handlers make scheduled deliveries and pickups every hour. Localized storage of materials was a big trend in past decades, but it is counterproductive as operator time, which is not used to produce product, impacts total flow time through the plant and thus incurs a plant cost penalty. Lean supplies a minimal amount of materials to the operations and places them so they are convenient for the operator to access, keeping operators at their station producing product.
- Material should flow on a first in, first out basis through packaging to shipping operations within a couple of hours. The operation doesn't need to be scheduled because packaging capacity is sufficient to process assembly peak volumes and mix.
- Optimize the packaging operation into an integrated cell with operators moving to machines when assembled product requires packing. In addition, transfer packaging supplies replenishment work to material handlers. These changes will reduce the number of operators on each shift, which will provide needed resources to staff shipping on the second shift and accelerate improvement projects.
- Implement error-proofing systems in packaging operations to prevent packaging and order fulfillment errors.

3. Change assembly operation scheduling practices (Figure 4.16, grey burst 3).

- Schedule case assembly and material will flow on a first in, first out basis through packaging since sufficient capacity is available to process peak volumes from assembly. This eliminates seven days of inventory between assembly and packaging. (Note: In Lean systems, only one operation is scheduled by production control. A scheduled operation is called a *pacemaker operation* as it sets the pace for other plant operations.) The current daily mix and volume variability of orders results in a significant challenge for scheduling to maintain the plant load level and meet customers' request dates. (Note: The Lean solution for resolving this apparent dilemma is level scheduling, which involves three principle concepts: Takt time, small lot sizes, and a period of time in which to accumulate orders for leveling volume.)

- Lean establishes an operational rhythm used to optimize resources and align cycle times of all operations to meet this rhythm. This rhythm is called *Takt time*. Takt time is customer demand divided by pacemaker operation available time. TCM average demand is 1,000,000 per day and the three shifts have 75,600 seconds available. 75,600 sec./1,000,000 units = .0756 seconds. A unit must be produced every .0756 seconds. Takt time is used to synchronize all operations to produce at the rate required while using the fewest possible resources.

- The product is packaged in 100 units per master carton. Ten thousand master cartons are packaged for shipment every day with orders for 10 master cartons representing 60 percent of shipments. Schedules are released in increments of 100 master cartons (mctn) or 12.6 minutes of assembly time (100 mctn × 100 units/ ctn × .0756 sec/unit = 756 sec or 12.6 minutes). This scheduling increment is called *pitch*. Short scheduling cycles are important to greatly reduce lead time and enable a level scheduling product mix.

- Order receipt until shipment lead time is 14 days, and adding 3 days delivery time results in a 17-day total order fulfillment lead time. Since project 2 will establish a FIFO flow through packaging and it will no longer be scheduled, the 8 days of assembled product inventory will be reduced to one day. This creates a potential reduction of 7 days in the order fulfillment lead time. Instead of reducing lead time by all 7 days, 4 days of this time will be used for accumulating orders to level the volume. Orders can be accumulated and leveled over the first 4 days after they are received, and then scheduled for assembly, packaging, and shipping. These processes will take 4 days, thus reliably meeting the planned 8-day plant lead time (Figure 4.16, see lead times for assembly, packaging, and shipping). This allows production control to level schedule volume over 4 days ensuring a consistent plant flow. If schedule volume for a day is below Takt time, a future day's orders are pulled ahead to level the schedule. These orders are produced, held in shipping, and released for shipment to meet the 8-day lead time. The combination of the 12.6-minute pitch to level product mix, 4-day volume schedule leveling time, and the occasional advance production results in consistently meeting the 8-day order fulfillment lead time and maintaining plant operations at a consistent level.

- Material will flow FIFO through packaging to shipping within two hours so shipping can aggregate orders and prepare them for shipment.

4. Schedule operation 1 based on assembly's supermarket pull signals when inventory trigger levels are reached. Materials flows FIFO through processes 2, 3, 4, and plating to the assembly material supermarket (Figure 4.16, grey burst 4).

- Create supermarkets to feed assembled and materials purchased from suppliers to production. Supermarkets should maintain only inventory needed to meet an operation's cycle time plus a level of safety stock. (Note: In process, supermarkets are used to support flow between two operations with different cycle times, changeover times, or available hours. Plating operations are an example with a cycle time of three days compared to assembly at 6 tenths of a second. The 15 days of plated inventory could be reduced simply by implementing a supermarket ahead of assembly with pull signals to authorize production from upstream operations. Supermarkets are not value added, but a necessary countermeasure until process stability and cycle times allow value streams to operate in true flow.) In this case, implementing a supermarket can reduce inventory from 15 days to 7 days. The total plant lead time through plating will then be 10 days—3 days of processing time plus 7 days of inventory. Because plating operations are a *monument* process, meaning it is not feasible in the short term to redesign the process to have inherently shorter cycle times, the entire FIFO flow time of 10 days will be treated on the value stream map as 10 days of inventory.

- Initiate Six Sigma DMAIC (define, measure, analyze, improve, control) projects to identify root causes of quality defects and implement permanent solutions.

5. Provide suppliers with daily demand and a 12-week demand forecast (Figure 4.16, grey burst 5), which will come from production control. Establish inventory supermarkets for raw materials supplied to operation 1, operation 4, and assembly with daily demand used to initiate delivery of more material. Reduce inventory, utilizing current weekly deliveries, to 10 days from the current 15 days and 20 days for raw materials.

6. Reduce moisture curing operation time (Figure 4.16, grey burst 6) by 6 days so material flows from process 4 through to assembly in less than 1 day. This can be accomplished by building smaller curing chambers that can be heated up and cooled down quickly. Complete a Six Sigma process definition project.

Improved process value-added time and lead times are shown on the step line at the bottom of the figure and the totals are shown in the bottom right-hand corner (Figure 4.16, grey burst 7). SIR scorecard supply chain improvement expected benefits are summarized in column labeled "F.S." or future state (Figure 4.16, grey burst 8).

The end state: Last, identified improvements and expected effects were summarized using a future-state value stream map (Figure 4.17). Future-state maps provide an end-state picture of the value stream when it is operating using only Lean practices.

As the future state is reviewed, expected benefits create excitement as TCM leadership is now able to see significant improvement possibilities beyond the year-one goals. The future-state map established goals for their longer-term vision (Figure 4.18). The financial benefit estimated for achieving the future state would place TCM as the indisputable market leader and fund strategic investments to ensure they could sustain the number one position. This additional homework—creating their future state—increased the team's confidence in achieving year-one goals, and they could see great opportunities well beyond the first year.

The leadership team could not wait to share its vision and action plan with their entire product development, marketing, sales, and manufacturing teams. There would be many barriers to overcome, but becoming market leaders again stimulated all executives to commit to leading their organization to achieve these challenging goals.

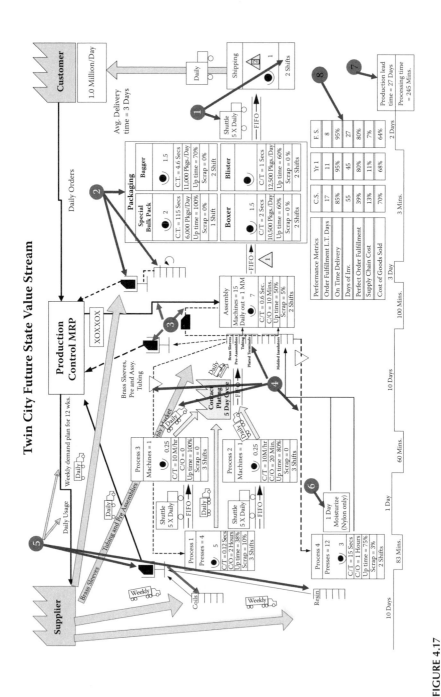

FIGURE 4.17

Twin City Manufacturing's future state value stream map illustrating improvement opportunities.

Twin City Manufacturing SIR Future State Goals

Key Perspectives Level 1 Metrics		Major Opportunity	Disadvantage	Average or Median	Advantage	Superior	Additional to Future State	1 yr. Plan
		Supply-Chain Performance Versus Custom Population						
Delivery Performance/ Quality	Delivery performance to request						+5% Pts. growth	5% + 5% Annual sales Incr.
	Perfect order fulfillment						Sustain	80%
Flexibility & Responsiveness	Upside production flexibility						Required to improve delivery performance to request	
	Order fulfillment lead time						Reduce 3.0 add'l days	7.5 Days
Cost	Supply-chain management cost						$10.4 M/yr	$5.2 M/yr
Working Capital	Cash-to-cash cycle time						10 add'ln days	10 Days
	Net asset turns						1.3 Turns $12.1 M	1.2 Turns $19.3 M
Total Benefit		First full year operating profit benefit					$19.0 M	$13.0 M
Included in S.C. management cost*		One time Inventory reduction					$12.0 M	$19.3

■ TCM position   ◆ Advantage   △ Superior

FIGURE 4.18
Twin City Manufacturing's SIR future state goals.

REFERENCES

Bossidy, Larry. *Confronting reality*. New York: Crown Press, 2004.

Graupp, Patrick, and Robert J. Wrona. *The TWI workbook*. New York: Productivity Press, 2006.

Porter, Michael. *Value chain*. New York: Free Press, 1985.

Porter, Michael, "What Is Strategy?" *Harvard Business Review* 74, 6 (1996): 61–78.

Shook, John, and Mike Rother. *Learning to see: Value stream mapping to add value and eliminate MUDA*. Cambridge, MA: Lean Enterprise Institute, 1999.

Treacy, Michael, and Fred Wiersema. *The discipline of market leaders*. Reading, MA: Addison Wesley, 1995.

5

The Role of the CEO and Leadership Team Implementing the Methodology

There are no success stories of radically improved results from transformational change that have not been championed by a company's top leaders. Leaders do things they understand and believe because failing may cost them their jobs. This raises a question: How many CEOs understand operational transformation methodologies well enough to bet their jobs and their companies on implementing one? The answer is, very few.

Leaders need to become familiar enough with improvement methodologies to lead them because today's fast-moving global markets require a continuous improvement process. Leaders who do not implement one, risk their jobs and the jobs of their team members.

TWIN CITY MANUFACTURING'S SUSTAINABLE IMPROVEMENT ROADMAP

Rick Hamilton set up a two-day off-site meeting with his team to develop their implementation plan. Rick knew from experience that his team needed to understand key implementation points for success as well as their leadership role in the process.

LEARNED FROM EXPERIENCE: PAUL

**SUCCESS BEGINS WITH A VISIONARY LEADER
WHO SETS A CLEAR GOAL AND THEN BACKS IT
UP WITH HIS OWN PERSONAL OVERSIGHT**

When GE's Jim McNerney joined 3M as the chairman and CEO in December 2000, 3M became a Six Sigma company. He personally championed Six Sigma by creating an executive leadership position reporting to him and a training and deployment infrastructure, and setting up an organization in each business that included a Six Sigma director, MBBs (Master Black Belts), and BBs (Black Belts). It was clear from the beginning that he had assigned the most talented people to the Six Sigma program.

The cause and vision were clear—3M needed to achieve consistent double-digit operating income and earnings-per-share growth. In 2000, 3M hadn't grown fast enough to achieve those goals so improving the cost and use of capital was the only option until growth rates improved. The plan for growth was to fund investments with part of the benefits from Six Sigma. This message was delivered consistently and everyone understood that providing our stockholders with attractive return was not optional.

From the beginning, Six Sigma was also promoted as an important leadership development experience, and soon all the most talented people wanted to participate in Six Sigma. All leaders at 3M during this period learned a great deal about leadership and the power of Six Sigma. During the four and a half years of the McNerney era at 3M, the stock price more than doubled, free cash flow more than doubled, and operating income increased more than 25 percent.

He started the meeting by presenting the following implementation program to get everyone on the same page.

1. **Three- to five-year implementation time horizon.** It takes three to five years to develop a mature supply chain that provides sustainable competitive advantage. Behavioral and cultural changes take time; for example, Lean system implementation takes two to three years. This doesn't mean significant results won't be generated along the

way, but sustainable change requires internalizing changes in thinking and practice, and this can only be accomplished with time.

The true test of leadership greatness is sustaining excellence at the highest level. Toyota has been perfecting their Toyota Production System for 50 years and has sustained quality, cost, service, and customer satisfaction leadership for two decades. Top executives at Toyota understand their operational system because they worked and contributed to making the system stronger. An important thing to learn from Toyota is that companies must have their own operational system, their own version of the Toyota Production System. This system provides a common language, structure, practice, and discipline, freeing the organization to focus on customers and improvement. This shared operational system also enables the retention of organizational knowledge and experience, preventing common problems that occur in many companies as one leadership generation passes to another. This sharing of retained knowledge prevents successive leadership generations from having to re-solve problems solved by previous leaders.

2. **Top executive team leadership**. Members of business organizations act primarily based on what they see from executive leadership and secondarily words heard. Leadership has six key implementation roles, which are described below.

- **Provide basic improvement process understanding**. Implementation of a sustainable supply chain improvement process demands leadership has at least a working-level knowledge of process. There is no evidence of significant success without active executive leadership, and this requires a working understanding of improvement processes and methodologies. How many times has an executive ordered inventory built assuming it would improve service? While it is possible that more inventory will address the root cause of poor service, 90 percent of the time this only creates more problems. Inventory obscures what is really happening in the process. This kind of behavior only demonstrates leadership's lack of basic supply chain understanding. Instead, leaders need to tell their organization that current service levels are unacceptable and customers need X level of service. They must ask for root cause analysis or what action is being taken to reach service goals. Leadership must act and communicate in a manner consistent with a basic understanding of supply chain and improvement methodologies.

- **Maintain Communication**. Communication is management's most important tool. A formalized communications process is important, but not a substitute for taking every opportunity to reinforce strategy, goals, successes, and failures. Larger organizations require compact messages to penetrate organizational layers and minimize misunderstanding as they cascade through organizational levels.

  Listening to every organizational level and checking its awareness, understanding, and commitment to goals and initiatives ensures leaders stay grounded in reality. This is a never-ending effort as each level of organizational understanding will lead to questions and concerns about what's next. Peeling layers of strategy, goals, and initiatives to their core is essential for achieving complete organizational understanding and requires committed, determined, persistent, and patient leadership.

- **Provide resources for success**. Initiatives that are only words from the leader are doomed to failure. Inertia in an organization must be overcome, and this only happens when commitment actions are aligned with management's words. Organizations must have skills, tools, dedicated professionals, and appropriate financial investments to be successful. Leaders must make sure their organization has these resources in place or implement actions to provide them.

- **Make decisions on resources necessary for success**. There is a tendency for project teams to ask for everything they believe might be needed. Leadership's role is to sort out essential resources required for success. This requires some challenging team assumptions and an open door for teams to come back if additional resources are required. Resources are always limited so leaders must provide support for success, recognizing that speed of implementation will depend on how many projects can be supported simultaneously.

- **Maintain operational review discipline**. The priority given to an initiative by an organization is directly linked to the priority demonstrated by their leaders. Leaders must be present, demand results, assist in overcoming barriers, keep the organization focused, praise good work, and constructively criticize and apply pressure to the 10 percent who aren't on board.

- **Stay in touch with reality.** Leaders must make opportunities to interact with all levels of the organization in order to communicate and check on the level of understanding and commitment to the initiatives. There is no substitute for the occasional deep dive into the organization to understand how well the leadership chain is communicating and implementing. The feedback to leadership from these deep dives is powerful as it helps the leadership chain understand that top management is fully committed and checking on progress.

  People naturally tend to do the things they want to do and think are important. If top leadership doesn't require a change in the priorities of the leadership chain, nothing will come of valuable initiatives.

- **Take timely action to resolve issues.** Nothing kills success like a leader who doesn't resolve issues on a timely basis and fails to take decisive action, resulting in demoralized team members who expect their leader to remove obstacles to improvement.

LEARNED FROM EXPERIENCE: PAUL

NEVER BE TOO BUSY TO TAKE A REALITY CHECK

During the first year that I ran the 3M Abrasives Division, quality problems were significant enough that my boss Harold Wiens and I had regular reviews with Jim McNerney. The discussion was direct and both Harold and Jim's great experience was invaluable to me. During one meeting, Jim said he had talked with sales people during a field visit, asking if they were confident problems were being fixed. Fortunately for me, they said yes. I learned that the CEO and chairman, who had many things to improve, occasionally "stuck his finger in the cake" to get a reality check. Audit, coach, and identify the next improvement!

Leaders who fail to act decisively will likely damage their credibility so severely that success becomes impossible. This includes holding their organization accountable for achieving results and modeling company values. It demands a high level of professional competence to succeed. Everything reasonable, which doesn't compromise end goals, must be done to give people sufficient time to get on board and acquire needed competencies, but in major transformations, everyone has to be on board. Experience tells us 10 percent of an organization will be unable or unwilling to get on board with transformational change. Consistently poor performers and cultural terrorists must be removed to sustain energy and commitment.

3. **Align organizational metrics.** Managing organizations by pitting one function or department against another was a common management practice in decades past. While this is no longer common, most organizations retained their conflicting functional metrics resulting in behavior similar to actually pitting departments against one another.

    Collaboration across organizations is accepted today as a best practice, but leaders seldom take time to make sure measurement and reward systems support collaboration. Metrics must be synchronized across organizations to optimize the enterprise rather than functional benefit.

    The Supply Chain Operations Reference (SCOR) linked metrics and Lean's Hoshin Kanri process are a valuable tools for aligning organizations, ensuring everyone's priorities are understood and all are pulling in the same direction.

LEARNED FROM EXPERIENCE: DAN

SUPPLY CHAIN OPERATIONAL METRICS MUST BE ALIGNED WITH CUSTOMER VALUE METRICS

While working on a supply chain assessment, an examination of the company's Key Performance Indicators revealed over twenty-five metrics updated weekly. They included all manner of machine and labor utilizations, yields, and waste. The weekly updating required one full-time person to gather and publish the data. Amazingly, none of the metrics pointed to the customer. In fact, no measures of on-time delivery, fill rate, or order cycle time existed. In this case, a short list of customer-focused metrics would have served the business much better.

4. **Develop a communications plan**. Communication keeps organizations informed, engaged, aligned. A structured communications process is a valuable element of transformational change because it

- maintains a disciplined schedule for regular communications,
- keeps team members informed on the state of the business,
- communicates improvement process successes and failures,
- gives team members an opportunity to question leadership and be heard, and
- provides an external view of the company from the perspective of customers and investors.

Communication is leadership's main tool for transformational change. Confusion, misunderstanding, anger, disagreement, and suspicion will all be present in an organization involved in transformational change. Regular communication from every level of leadership is required to acknowledge people's feelings and at the same time reinforce the bigger cause for change requiring continued commitment.

Ninety percent of people are able to accept and live with things they don't completely agree with as long as they have had an opportunity to be heard and feel respected. Allowing people to keep their own feelings about change also enables them to change their opinion when they see growing company success. Nothing prevents people from changing their point of view more than resentment and anger generated from feelings that have been disrespected and not heard.

- Transformational change is about building a wave of positive organizational support, which naturally overcomes resistance of all but the last 10 percent who will never get on board. This last 10 percent will be resolved as they leave, accept change, or are asked to leave because they are no longer aligned with the organization.
- A formal communications plan has four elements:
  - Initial CEO communication of the vision to the entire organization
  - Cascading communications throughout an entire organization to make sure that everyone understands key messages and that they will be provided with training for implementation
  - Quarterly organizationwide communication meetings

- Periodic assessments by the Human Resources or Communications Department to provide feedback on leadership's performance and organizational understanding, acceptance, and commitment.

5. **Manage implementation through a program management office.** No one would consider building a bridge, road, or plant without a strong project leader and dedicated project managers for the major components. Implementing a companywide supply chain improvement initiative is more complex than building a new plant. It requires sufficient structure and skills to be successful.

   Program office management and project management are not strong inherent skills in most organizations, except in the specific groups that build plants, design and implement new process equipment, or implement IT systems. Success requires an overall program leader who is an accomplished project manager and organizational guide.

   Top leadership must be supported by dedicated project managers and a supply chain specialist. There is no single organizational model that fits all businesses or projects, but there are universally required skills and leadership capabilities. Leaders must understand the skills required for improvement so they can define appropriate resources and structure to fit their program.

6. **Build the project plan.** Creating a vision using benchmarking and value stream mapping information establishes the improvement goals and priority projects. Project leaders must establish project plans to meet the performance improvement goals and identify significant stages of progress or milestones. These project milestones are the focus of monthly project reviews.

   Failure to meet milestones requires immediate intervention with actions to get projects back on track. Frequently project leaders spend hours completing detailed project plans with all activities using project-planning software. They often focus on activity tracking and rescheduling, assuming that this is project management. Unfortunately, this common practice usually leads to failure. Project managers must do several things for the project to succeed:

   - Define the project, its scope, and deliverables
   - Establish and track project milestones
   - Understand project risk related to each milestone and have contingencies prepared if failure appears probable

- Understand milestone critical paths, which can not be off schedule, or projects will not achieve their goal
- Conduct regular monthly project reviews

Executive leaders do not need to be project experts but they must question project leaders about these five points. Only constant follow up will ensure expected results and early detection of potential failures while time is still available to get back on schedule.

7. **Plan how to overcome resistance to change.** Experience shows human resistance to change is the greatest barrier to how quickly supply chain improvement can be implemented. This issue has such a great effect on supply chain projects because improvement is achieved only when people do their jobs in a different way.

Project leadership, supply chain professional competencies, and committed top leadership champions are required for success, but eliminating people's resistance to change is always the most significant challenge. This is why the executive's role as project champion is a critical success factor for all project teams. Top leaders must take an active role in continually communicating the vision and making a compelling case for change to all organizational levels. Tools such

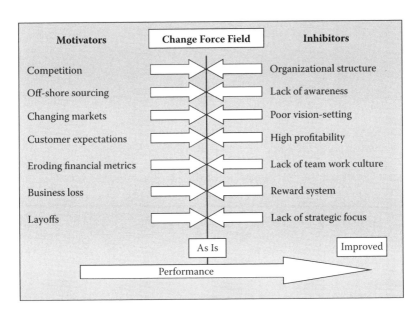

FIGURE 5.1
The change force field.

as the change force field (Figure 5.1) can be used at all organizational levels to help understand and overcome resistance to change.

Top leadership also needs to recognize three groups of people in the organization: early adaptors, observers, and hard-core resistors. These three groups will be present in every transformational change. Leadership needs to take a specific approach to each group.

Early adaptors need to be reinforced and encouraged to become active change agents. This is normally very easy as they are inclined to support change that improves business results. Observers are the pivotal group for success. Leadership must work very hard to get observers to get off the fence and join with the early adaptors. Getting observers moved to active supporters is critical to building majority organization consensus, which gives legitimacy to change. Leaders must be patiently firm with strong resistors. Many of them have what they think are legitimate reservations but will eventually get on board. The remaining resistors and organizational terrorists will frequently opt out when they feel pressure from peers, but, if they don't, leadership must step in and take action to remove them.

8. **Conduct regular operational reviews at all levels.** This review process must occur at all levels of the organization with greater frequency as it moves from top level operational performance reviews to daily shop floor reviews.

LEARNED FROM EXPERIENCE: PAUL

STANDARDIZE WORK AT ALL LEVELS

Along with 3M manufacturing leadership, Rick Harris of Harris Lean Systems conducted operational Lean reviews with all 60 facility managers in North America, with 6 to 10 facilities per session, held every four months. Harris devoted one of the sessions to teaching standardized work for managers.

Daily shop floor reviews are essential for maintaining operational discipline, continuous improvement, and employee development. Lean, for example, is a people- and leadership-based process with layered audit control plans. Operators, floor supervisors, and area managers have a daily standardized work routine to audit certain areas. Plant managers spend their first couple of hours each day reviewing shop floor operations to audit, coach, and identify the next area of improvement.

- **Audit**: Leaders at all levels audit an area others have audited, ensuring real accountability because everyone knows that at some point their work is inspected. Audits are a preventive and act as an early detection system by identifying small deviations that may cause quality, service, safety, or cost failure if not corrected.

- **Coach**: Lean teaches practitioners to see with *new eyes* and seek the perfection that is fundamental to continuous improvement. Tools and methods obviously assist in this process, but a greatly increased sensitivity to waste and its sources changes managers' thinking. This skill needs to be coached and nurtured every day by questioning, for example, why the hourly production target wasn't achieved, or why something is done in a particular way. Why, why, why, why? This drive to understand processes, identify root causes, and implement solutions is also an opportunity for leadership to share their knowledge and experience.

- **Identify next levels of improvement**: In addition to auditing and coaching, time must be spent observing operations, not only to understand the details of a particular process, but also to see how the entire system is functioning. This experience reinforces something most leaders know (but do not do), which is that time dedicated to operational reviews is critical to both process improvement and leadership development. Many times reviews turn into a search for the guilty and punishment for the innocent. Leaders frequently want to show their knowledge, but instead demonstrate their arrogance and ignorance about their supply chain. Leaders must constantly remind themselves that they must also be learners.

9. **Build and maintain momentum by achieving early results.** Nothing provides energy, credibility, and confidence to an organization like success. Early benefit is an important criterion in project selection because it provides organizational reinforcement. Early success is also crucial to overcoming resistance, convincing uncommitted observers to get on board thus isolating hard-core change resistors.

10. **Relentlessly pursue the end state.** Organizations are frequently critical of their leadership for focusing on only the short term. This has become a greater leadership challenge as investment analysts push for continuous quarter-by-quarter improvement in financial performance. Leaders must continually remind the organization of the reasons for the improvement journey and that achievement of short-term benefit is an important first step toward achieving the long-term visions. Leaders must model a focused commitment to end-state achievement. This builds their credibility for dealing with the inevitable unexpected events that require short-term reprioritization of projects to sustain overall improvement. These events will be viewed in their proper perspective once an organization has experienced sustained leadership commitment to their transformational end-state journey.

Factors Affecting the Success of an Implementation Plan

The success of supply chain improvement depends on applying lessons learned by incorporating them into implementation plans. These success factors should be used as an assessment tool for plan completeness. Following is a checklist for successful implementation plans:

- Top executive leadership as its champion
- A vision and cause created by the CEO
- Top talent as resources
- All employees—including executives—trained and contributing to projects
- Established cost, cash, and growth targets
- Measurable hard savings against leadership targets; soft savings should count only when directly connected to future strategic goals
- Improvement expectations integrated into every operational review
- Disciplined project scope to ensure completion in four to six months
- Using Six Sigma only when root causes are unknown and difficult to determine
- Coaching from statistical experts
- Project leaders, Master Black Belts, and Black Belts held accountable for project results by leadership champions
- Stakeholders who buy into solutions
- Rigorous control plans measured by an independent organization
- Operating budgets and plans that, after one year, factor in a percentage of the expected improvement process benefits (30 to 50 percent)

TWIN CITY MANUFACTURING'S IMPLEMENTATION PROGRAM

The Twin City Manufacturing leadership team was eager to move into implementation. Their vision was set, their performance improvement priorities had been validated by customers, and first improvement cycle projects were defined. Rick knew that aligning organizational performance review metrics, establishing project implementation leadership resources, preparing for resistance, and agreeing on communications plans would be good investments in overall implementation speed.

The Twin City executives learned, through SCOR training, how Level 1 through Level 3 metrics were directly linked and effectively enabled alignment of supply chain performance objectives throughout their organization.

Improving service (defined by their scorecard metrics) to an advantage position was their highest priority. The executives understood that this did not mean that budgets and other cost-related goals could be ignored; instead it meant that when one of their teams faced a decision, cost-related constraints that conflicted with meeting service goals should be discussed so teams and leaders collectively resolve the issue.

There was also an implied understanding costs would improve from efficiencies gained as they implemented their six value stream programs. Rick and his executive team reviewed each key operating department using the SCOR Levels 1 to 3 metrics and Hoshin Kanri to make sure every operation was on the same page by eliminating all conflicting metrics. With metric alignment complete, they organized the project structure. The plant process engineering manager was named the Lean implementation manager because she had significant project implementation experience. Four factory managers were assigned as leadership team members responsible for implementing the seven projects. Three process engineers were assigned full time to project implementation and more resources would be added as productivity improved and key operators could be added full time. Force field analysis was done at three levels:

1. Corporately, by focusing on cultural barriers
2. By functional departments to understand how all would view planned transformation and its effect on their areas
3. By project to understand how the groups involved might resist implementation

Examining their culture and its strongly held organization views, they came up with four strongly held beliefs that would need to be changed or modified to enable transformational change to be embraced (see Figure 5.2).

Next, six motivating forces that could be used to overcome current belief barriers were identified. Leadership team members saw what was needed but were unsure how to successfully make these changes to move their transformation ahead. Rick Hamilton drew on his experience and shared with his team the five key leadership communication principles needed for successfully persuading an organization to modify its beliefs and embrace significant change:

1. Respect and reinforce past organizational successes
2. Define what made successes possible
3. Share the goals and objectives required for continued success

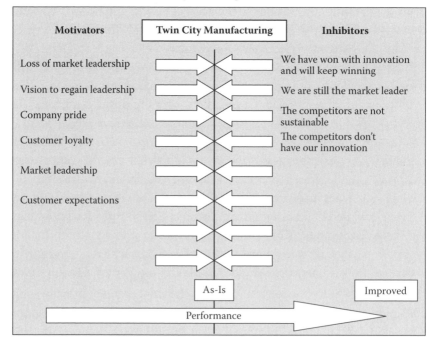

FIGURE 5.2
The Twin City Manufacturing change force field.

4. Explain the benefits of achieving organizational goals and objectives
5. Communicate action plans and accountability for implementation

Application of these five principles maintains focus on moving forward and using past successes to create forward momentum for implementing change. Applying force field analysis and Hamilton's five communications principles, the team created its communications plan content. Rick could see his team was moving from having significant reservations to being excited about getting started with communications. They saw a positive approach to co-opting their organizations to join the transformational journey.

The marketing and communications executive shared key points of good communication plans and leadership's role in the process. The following communications expectations were agreed upon:

- Communication of the initial vision by Rick was scheduled in a series of meetings with all company team members.
- Each executive team member would follow up with communications through the entire organization, making sure all understood the message how it would impact their function and training plans.
- Quarterly follow-up communications meetings were scheduled by all executive team members with an agenda and expectation of publishing a summary of results to all executive team members.
- The Human Resources department would randomly sample 10 percent of the organization each quarter to assess their views on leadership and understanding, acceptance, and commitment to the improvement initiative.
- Every six months the national sales manager would survey key customers by personal interview. This survey would include owners, sales managers, logistics managers, procurement managers along with operational-level people in each function.

The executives now felt completely ready to push the button and begin. The vision was clear; customers validated the improvement priorities, the first cycle of projects had been identified, and a plan to overcome organizational resistance to change and a communications plan were both in place. It was time to get the entire organization up to speed, on board, and committed to making the necessary changes.

Over the following two weeks, round one of communications was completed, and everyone had an opportunity to express doubts, concerns, and criticisms.

With initial communications complete, Rick's leadership team reviewed their original change acceptance plan to consider feedback from all levels of management on issues and concerns voiced during the initial communications meetings. They reviewed the companywide force field analysis and concluded that no significant changes were needed, but they reminded themselves to use the five leadership communication principles and stay aligned with the communication plan.

It was time to get everyone fully engaged in moving implementation forward. They invited Susan Zoelzer, engineering manager, and her implementation team to join them in a two-day workshop to start implementation. The first half day focused on reviewing benchmarking results, customer value analysis and value stream maps, improvement goals, and implementation plans to be sure implementation team members were comfortable discussing the vision with their colleagues. Rick recommended they carefully consider their organizational capacity for change and resources to complete improvement projects. After some discussion, they concluded that given their organization's maximum capacity, they could complete improvements through project 3 in 90 days. Reviewing each project led to the establishment of the following three-month goals (Figure 5.4):

1. Reduce order fulfillment lead time from 17 days to 11 days
2. Increase on-time delivery service from 85 percent to 90 percent
3. Decrease number of days of inventory from 55 to 49
4. Increase perfect order fulfillment from 39 percent to 70 percent
5. Reduce supply chain cost from 14 percent to 13 percent
6. Reduce cost of goods sold from 70 percent to 69 percent

Once agreed-upon goals for the next three months were established, it was time for Susan's team to take ownership of plan implementation.

The remainder of the first day focused on a detailed review of value stream maps and improvement projects one, two, and three (Figure 5.3), which were selected because they would be felt by customers and provide early successes that would be visible across the company. In addition, these projects would take maximum effort by the entire organization; it was Twin City Manufacturing's limit.

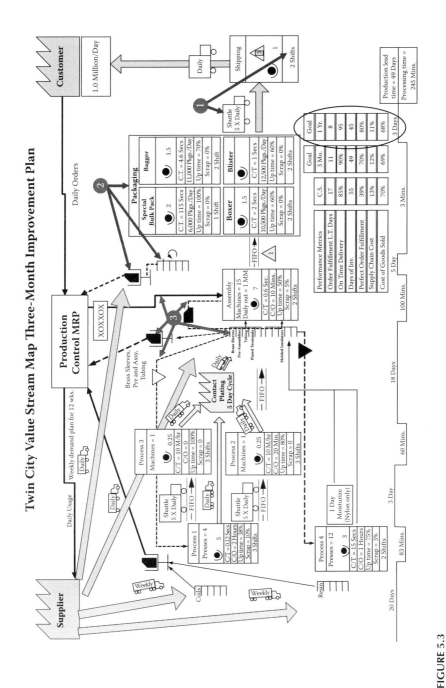

FIGURE 5.3

Twin City Manufacturing's three-month improvement plan.

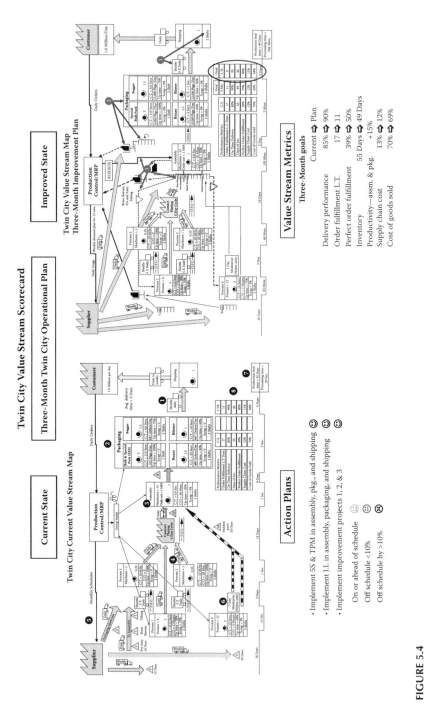

FIGURE 5.4
Twin City Manufacturing's value stream scorecard, three-month operational review.

Step 1 for Lean to be successful is to establish stability based on a foundation of order, discipline, standardization, and reliability. This foundation requires the implementation of 5S (Sort, Set in order, Straighten, Shine, and Sustain), Total Productive Maintenance (TPM), a key element of Lean stabilization (the methodology was documented by Seiichi Nakajima in his 1984 book *TPM*), standard work instructions, and cell optimization. Rick personally trained the implementation team on 5S and held weekly coaching meetings with the team until all members were comfortable with implementation.

TPM is an equipment maintenance methodology that ensures high reliability and availability of equipment in a very cost-effective manner by involving all plant team members. Fortunately, Susan Zoelzer, who had recently attended a maintenance seminar, was energized by the thought of being supported to implement TPM at TCM. The goal was zero breakdowns.

TPM deals with machine stability while Training Within Industry (TWI), a tried and true method for standardizing work instructions, stabilizes work methods and minimizes team member variability in completing each work task. TWI was a U.S. government program, established during World War II, and developed and refined for five years as hundreds of thousands of workers were trained. After the war it was used in Japan, which had lost many skilled workers. TWI was vitally important in enabling the rapid development of a well-trained manufacturing workforce in Japan. Toyota was an early adaptor of TWI as the foundation for continuous improvement. Earlier, Rick Hamilton had assigned Charlie Dubey (the human resources executive) to take ownership of providing Job Instruction (JI) training and establishing a center of excellence to sustain it. JI is one of three training components of TWI.

TWI has three components: Job Instruction (JI) for training workers to perform a specific job; Job Methods (JM) for improving safety, productivity, and quality of a job; and Job Relations (JR) to prepare employees to work with others. Charlie supplied each of the implementation team members with *The TWI Workbook* (2006) written by Patrick Graupp and Robert J. Wrona. The managers and supervisors from the shipping, packaging, and assembly areas were invited to join the project team in learning TWI during a two-week, two-hour-a-day training class.

JI focuses on only the essential job information and knowledge a person needs to perform the job. The job is broken down into three areas: (1) important steps, (2) key points about each step, and (3) reasons for each step. Often more detailed procedures are created that are used as input for creating JI, but they are often not easy for shop floor team members to use. JM and JR will be deployed later when team members can immediately apply them.

Cell optimization is the final methodology required to achieve stabilization; it focuses on optimizing the value-added work performed by operators and ensures the cell operates at a cycle time slightly less than Takt time (customer demand divided by available production time expressed in seconds per part). This ensures the cells can support flow and pull at the rate of customer demand. The second day was spent reviewing project resources, potential barriers, implementation risk, and contingency plans, and establishing operational review dates and agendas.

Implementation of Priority Projects

Susan and her team put together implementation plans for value stream projects one, two, and three. These three projects would improve delivery performance, perfect order flexibility, and supply chain response time, closing benchmarked performance gaps.

Before implementing priority projects, foundational projects—5S, TPM, TWI, and cell optimization—had to be implemented to create basic order and consistency in performing each job, as well as to engage shop floor team members in continuous improvement. They had to be implemented, operationally, in the same order as the initial three project implementations. Each project was reviewed and if it could not be completed in three months, it was broken down into subprojects with a clear scope, objectives, and resources. Susan summarized their plan as follows:

1. Operational environment and discipline will be established first through implementation of 5S, TPM, JI, and cell optimization in shipping, packaging, and assembly.
2. Shuttle frequency of product from packaging to shipping operations will be immediately increased to one every hour and two shifts in shipping will be scheduled to support same-day shipment of second shift–produced product (value stream improvement project 1).
3. Packaging operation implementation sequence (value stream improvement project 2) will be established.

   • Perform packaging operation cell optimization.

- Implement error-proofing systems to prevent packaging and order fulfillment errors.
- Eliminate practice of operators replenishing packaging materials by establishing central supermarket and having material handlers make scheduled deliveries every hour.
- Provide daily usage to packaging supply vendors and receive daily replenishments.
- Stop scheduling packaging operations and flow materials (FIFO, first in, first out) through packaging to shipping.

4. Change assembly operation scheduling practices and apply Six Sigma to resolve current quality issues (value stream improvement project 3)

- Establish assembly as the pacemaker operation using level scheduling techniques to efficiently make mix and volume requirements
  - Establish Takt time.
  - Implement scheduling with a 12.6-minute pitch (10 master cartons).
  - Implement level scheduling of customer orders by utilizing the first four days and releasing on the fifth day to meet the five-day order processing lead time.
- Initiate Six Sigma DMAIC (define, measure, analyze, improve, control) projects to identify root causes of quality defects and implement permanent solutions.

The first order of business was training project implementation team members and shop floor team members in shipping, packaging, and assembly in 5S, TPM, JI, and cell optimization. Each team leader was assigned responsibility for implementing it in his or her area. They were to meet once per week to share what they learned, critique one of their areas to help the leaders make progress, and keep a consistent approach to 5S across the plant. An excellent resource for training shop floor team members on many of the Lean tools and practices is *Just-in-Time for Operators* (1998), which was written and illustrated for shop floor training.

The department managers made daily walks through their areas each morning to audit 5S and TPM compliance. This is a very important step because sustaining Lean system continuous improvement depends on active management shop floor involvement to audit standardized work, achieve schedules, and maintain safety. Three months later the teams had completed their projects and Lean was beginning to take hold in the plant. Results were coming ahead of expectations and shop floor team members were engaged because management finally solved some basic job-related issues.

The first executive team review was scheduled after three months of implementation, and executive team members all arrived early for their first Sustainable Improvement Roadmap (SIR) review. There was a sense of anticipation as they all felt very good about what had been accomplished. The entire organization had responded enthusiastically to their call to regain market leadership. Implementation of projects 1, 2, and 3 was completed ahead of schedule, and they were hoping Rick Hamilton would acknowledge this success.

Rick reviewed the agenda and his expectations from the meeting: a review of SIR scorecard progress and value stream improvement status would be completed, scorecard goals and value stream projects for the next three months would be discussed, and key action items would be summarized.

Quarterly SIR progress reviews were jointly presented by Operations Vice President Eaton Oesterlein and CFO Fred Gilligan. Fred reviewed the SIR scorecard (Figure 5.5), and minimum progress to plan was 100 percent.

Twin Cities Manufacturing SIR Scorecard
3-Month Operational Review

Key Perspectives	SCOR Level 1 Metrics	Major Opportunity	Disadvantage	Average or Median	Advantage	Superior	1 yr. Plan
Delivery Performance/ Quality	Delivery performance to request			140% 100%			5% + 5% $3.9 M/yr + $3.9 M yr.1
	Perfect order fulfillment				100%		+ 31% pts*
Flexibility & Responsiveness	Upside production flexibility			100%			Required capability
	Order fulfillment lead time (MTO)			100%			−7.5 Days
Cost	Supply-chain management cost			100%			−2.0% $5.2 M/yr
Working Capital	Cash-to-cash cycle time		100%				10 Day reduction
	Net asset turns						1.2 Turns $19.3 M Inv reduction.
Total Benefit Included in S.C. management cost*		First full year operating profit benefit					$13.0 M
		One time inventory reduction					$19.3 M

Supply-Chain Performance Versus Custom Population ☆

■ TCM position ▽ TCM progress ◆ Advantage △ Superior

FIGURE 5.5
SIR scorecard.

1. Delivery performance to request date reached 92 percent versus the goal of 90 percent. This resulted from shorter assembly through shipment flow time and implementation of their new level scheduling process.
2. Order fulfillment lead time was right on target with a reduction of 6 days to a plant lead time of 8 days and total lead time of 11 days as a result of implementation of a single scheduling point and FIFO flow from assembly through shipping.
3. Perfect order fulfillment improved from 39 to 50 percent based on improved delivery performance and reductions in shipping errors.
4. Upside production flexibility was improved by 20 days (from 40 days to 20 days), creating an advantage position, through implementation of cross-training of operators, operator certification, and creation of a part-time work team willing to flex their hours from a minimum of 20 per week to a maximum of 40 hours per week.

The scorecard reflected great progress on their value stream, as all of the goals established for the three-month period were met or exceeded. Odair Brazil, sales vice president, interrupted the presentation, starting his comments by acknowledging that 90 percent of the time he is very critical of operations because they cause so many problems for customers, but today he had to admit that customers were asking sales people, "What is going on at Twin City?" They were experiencing better delivery reliability and fewer errors. Sales representatives were receiving many questions from customers who wanted to know if the improvement was just a coincidence or a permanent change in delivery and quality performance. The sales force, still dubious about improvement sustainability, explained that TCM was putting effort into supply chain improvement, but they were reluctant to promise it would continue. Their credibility had suffered over the years from poor performance, so they were not going sell improvements too hard until they saw a longer period of improvement. His final comment was, "I am going to send an e-mail to our entire sales force today, encouraging them to believe and sell these improvements to customers." Eaton was in shock for a few seconds. He had rarely heard a positive comment from Odair about his operations. After taking a moment to recover, he took over and presented the value stream scorecard (Figure 5.6). The group knew there had been good progress, but was surprised by the level of progress after just three months. They felt the shop floor team member

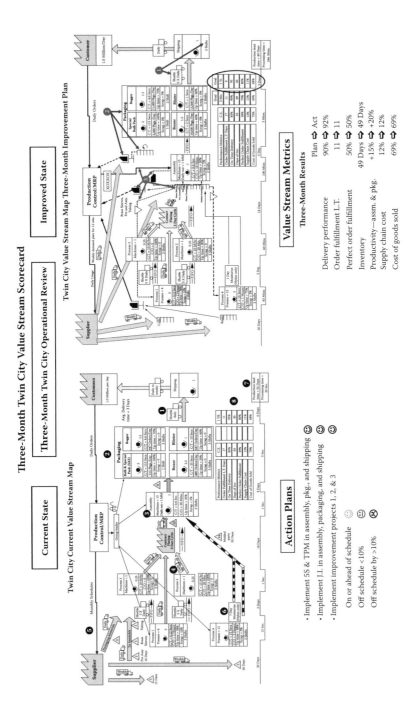

FIGURE 5.6

Twin City Manufacturing's value stream scorecard, three-month operational review.

enthusiasm from lunchroom conversations and shop floor visits. Now they understood why everyone was so energized: Results were reinforcing changes being made from improvement project implementation. Shop floor team members routinely commented that management was finally listening. Long-standing issues that interfered with getting things done right were being solved every day.

Eaton reviewed only those results that had not shown up on the SIR scorecard: inventory, productivity, and cost of goods sold.

Implementation of JI standard work, TPM, 5S, error proofing, and optimizing work cells produced significant improvement in safety and quality and resulted in a 20 percent productivity gain. These changes also improved product flow and stabilized operations resulting in improved production output consistency. Improved flow and shorter cycle times were critical to successful implementation of FIFO flow from assembly through packaging. An assembly materials inventory supermarket was created as a countermeasure to accommodate imbalances between assembly operations cycle times and the cycle times of upstream processes that provide assembly materials. This supermarket smoothed out volume demand on upstream operations, resulting in a six-day reduction in assembly materials inventory. The improved speed through the plant and productivity improvements contributed to reducing the cost of goods sold by one percentage point. Odair couldn't contain himself: "Those are great results, but I have a question: You guys aren't just cutting inventory, which will start to hurt service, are you?" "No," replied Eaton, "you can be confident that won't happen. Everyone has been trained and is held accountable for making sure customers are always protected when changes are made. Inventory reduction is possible because we are producing exactly what customers order and replenishing parts based on actual consumption."

Moving on with his presentation, Eaton displayed the three-month improvement plan value stream map, it showed a three-day cycle time achieved for assembly and packaging product. He explained the actual improvement had been six days, but three of those days had been taken by scheduling to accumulate customer orders to level the schedule before the orders were released to assembly in time to meet the ship date. "Does this new level scheduling mean we can quit wasting our time with Sales and Operations Planning meetings each month?" retorted Odair. "Certainly not," responded Eaton. "We can stop spending time on near-term demand as our system is now much more flexible and able to handle short-term variation. The meetings can be more valuable, focusing on future expectations from customers, market place events, responding to unplanned opportunities, and taking actions to gain additional business at key customers." Odair commented, "Now that sounds like value-added to me. When do we start this new agenda?" Eaton answered, "We are starting this month and will measure ourselves by sales to our major customers." Odair looked at Rick Hamilton and joked, "I must have come to work at the wrong place this morning. This all sounds like my dream come true. Operations is finally going to help us sell and we won't have to carry them around on our backs anymore. Did I die and go to heaven?" The room burst out in laughter as Rick looked at him and said, "You are right. Starting today, this is a new company, and the customer comes first."

Eaton next presented the six-month plan (Figure 5.7) and reviewed specific projects (Figure 5.8). Team members sat in silence, stunned by what they saw. Eaton explained that he had worked with their improvement team and consulted with Rick about taking an aggressive view of accelerating improvement in the six-month plan. They all agreed; they would share the risk of coming up short but were all committed to the plan. The plan presented would achieve year-one goals in six months. If this could be done, they would be able to regain their market leadership in one year—nothing short of a miracle.

Rick coached, challenged, and encouraged the group by saying, "This is just the beginning. With relentless commitment to perfection, there is no limit to what Twin City Manufacturing can achieve. It is up to us." Eaton had taken notes of the action items and presented a summary:

1. Three-month progress indicates improvement can be made at a rate faster than anticipated. Susan Zoelzer and her team will be challenged to complete remaining year-one projects in the next three months.
2. Charlie Dubey will prepare a companywide communication of three-month progress, the accelerated plan for the next three months, and customer feedback.
3. Eaton Oesterlein will focus sales and operations planning meetings aimed at increasing sales at key customers.
4. Odair Brasil will send customer communications to all sales representatives explaining improvements made and reinforcing commitment to adding customer value.

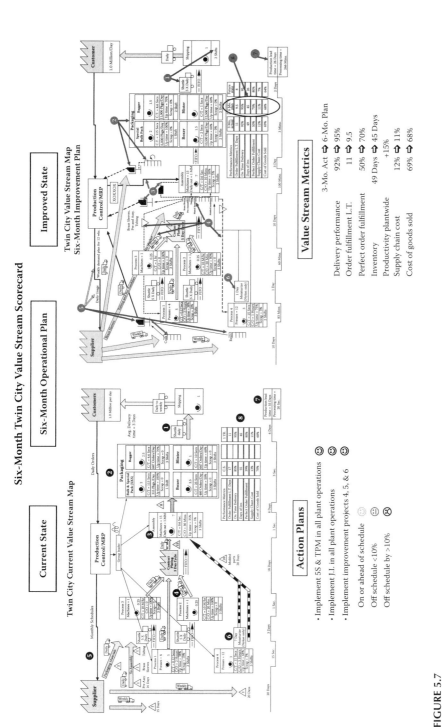

FIGURE 5.7
Twin City Manufacturing's value stream scorecard, six-month operational plan.

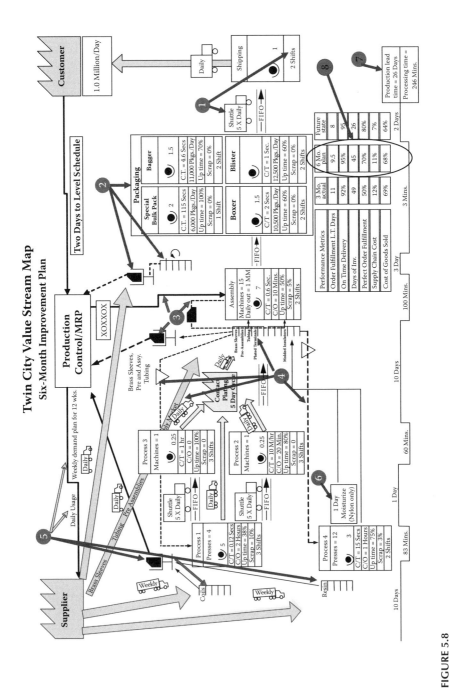

FIGURE 5.8

Twin City Manufacturing value stream map: six-month improvement plan.

5. Odair Brasil will complete EVA (Economic Value Added) feedback of improvement with key customers.

Susan Zoelzer and her team accepted the challenge to complete year one projects in six months and felt motivated by their executives' confidence in their work. Project teams worked all out during the next three months and progress went very well—the total plant was now on board with Lean and enthusiastic about contributing to regaining the company's market leadership.

The projects to implement 5S, TPM, and JI plantwide were quickly accomplished as teams and supervisors didn't want to be left behind and were already applying them in their own areas. Because supervisors were taking ownership of these projects, Susan and her team could concentrate on projects 4, 5, and 6. Project 4 was to eliminate the scheduling of operations 1 through 4 by using Kanban signals from the assembly supermarket to authorize making product at operations 1 and 4. The materials produced from operation 1 would flow FIFO through operations 2, 3, and plating into the assembly supermarket.

Their first challenge was the two-hour changeover time at operation 1. To flow the mix through the downstream operation to assembly, changeover time had to be 20 minutes or less. Rick taught Susan Zoelzer, her team, and the maintenance supervisors how to apply SMED (Single Minute Exchange of Dies) methodology, a process developed by Shigeo Shingo and well-publicized in his book, *A Revolution in Manufacturing: The SMED System* (1985). Applying this methodology, a cross-functional team identified opportunities to reduce changeover time by one hour taking work currently done within the changeover process and having it done either before or simultaneously during changeover by another operator. Team maintenance technicians and machinists identified changes they could make to set up tooling the machine to reduce an additional 45 minutes. This was ideal because the 15-minute setup time was less than the 20-minute set-up at operation 2, which meant they could cycle operation 1 so that operation 2 would be supplied on a FIFO basis and inventory would not be sitting between them to buffer operation 2. Improvements were implemented within 40 days and after 60 days flow from operation 1 through to assembly was working perfectly.

Operation 4 was an entirely different challenge. Molding operations were very flexible because molds could be quickly changed, and the process could be tuned to making a new part in less than 15 minutes. Curing oven design, which required large batches, was the constraint. It took a long time to fill the oven with parts, get it up to temperature, and after curing, get it back down to ambient temperature and remove the parts. Actual curing time was only 18 hours, so engineering was challenged to come up with an inexpensive process requiring only one day. The current process had evolved by trial and error over the years, so process conditions were not well understood. This became the first project for engineering.

Six Sigma DMAIC was used to define the best process conditions and ranges for all key variables. The outcomes of designed experiments were a surprise. First, material curing was complete enough after only 12 hours. This meant that it was technically feasible to get the ovens up to temperature, cure parts, and cool down to ambient temperatures in less than 24 hours. Second, reducing the time required to heat material and cool it down had no detrimental effect on its performance. These two facts led the engineers to develop a concept for smaller ovens capable of rapidly reaching curing temperatures, and with enough exhaust and cooling capability, to bring material back to ambient temperature in an hour. The result was 6 small curing operations able to complete curing in less than 24 hours. All the materials needed for the new curing process were commercially available, so they were built by plant machinists and installed before the quarter's end, just in time to have results for the next review.

Implementation team members assigned to reducing supplier inventory had underestimated the challenge of getting key suppliers on board. They were not resisting change, but it was all new to their organizations and it took them time to really understand and embrace Lean. Projects were moving forward as the next review approached, but only partial results would be achieved and another month was required to completely achieve project inventory goals.

Susan and her team were eager to put together the review update and hoped their slight miss on supplier projects wouldn't detract from great overall progress and everyone's extremely hard work. They also wanted to see how SIR scorecard metrics improved as a result of their work, but for this, they would have to wait until the meeting.

Eaton and Fred put together the SIR scorecard and value stream project update. They were very pleased with the plant's progress despite missing on supplier material inventories goals. They were sure Rick and the others would be pleased.

At the six-month review meeting, Rick announced they would spend an hour at every review on the shop floor in addition to their update presentations. Eaton Oesterlien presented project team progress since the last review (Figure 5.9). The value stream metrics showed order fulfillment lead time, perfect order fulfillment, days of inventory, productivity, supply chain cost, and cost of goods sold exceeded targets, while delivery performance achieved its target.

The 5S, TPM, and JI projects had gone smoothly, which was fundamental to the implementation team's success because it allowed project teams to focus entirely on projects 4, 5, and 6. Shop floor team members had spread the word plantwide that management was finally listening; productivity, quality, and service had improved; and jobs were easier and safer, which motivated everyone to get engaged in Lean. Supervisors from assembly and packaging were trained in other plant operations in 5S, TPM, and JI, creating a self-sustaining capability. Project 4 (see Figure 5.10), implementing assembly supermarket Kanban signals to schedule operation 1 (cut to width) with FIFO flow through operations 2, 3, and plating had gone smoothly once the setup time on operation 1 was reduced to 15 minutes.

Project 6, reducing the cycle time of insulator molding from seven days to one day, was completed and working successfully. Six smaller curing thermal chambers had been installed and cycle time was now less than 24 hours. With shorter process cycle times, molded insulator assembly materials supermarket inventory was minimized and the operation could respond to required daily assembly mix changes.

Project 5 was not completely successful. It took longer than expected to get supplier organizations to understand, embrace Lean, and change the materials replenishment process. Although the project was off schedule, each day's inventory goal was still exceeded because the SIR six-month goal was to maintain 45 days of inventory, which had already been achieved. Working with suppliers, project 5 would be completed within 30 days.

Rick Hamilton summarized his observations and then coached the group on his expectations: "We didn't achieve every goal or every project on time, but I would rather achieve 90 percent of aggressive stretch goals than 100 percent of small incremental goals. So, congratulations to Susan, her team, and our entire plant. We now have our Lean System basics in place and I mean basics, we have a lot of hard work to do now to accelerate our improvement rate."

Fred Gilligan presented the SIR scorecard update (Figure 5.11). He was always a believer in Lean and results after 6 months just confirmed his

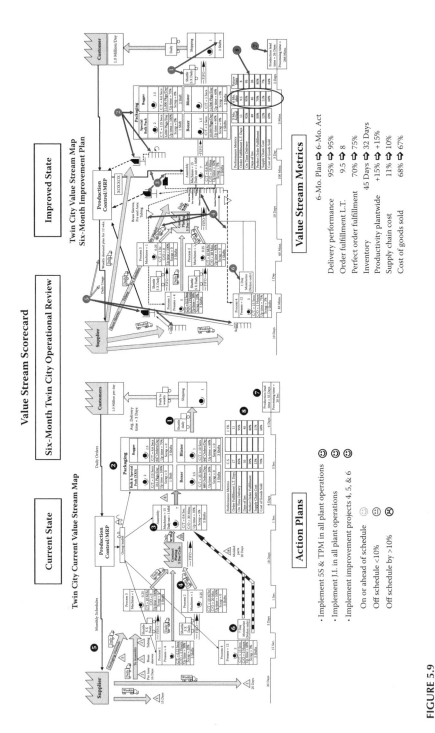

FIGURE 5.9

Twin City Manufacturing value stream scorecard, six-month operational review.

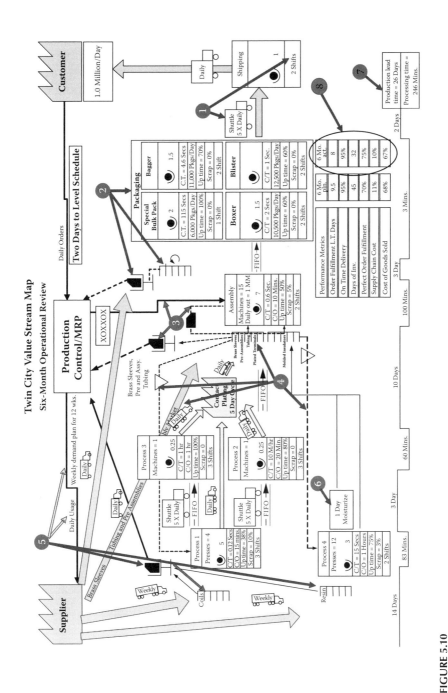

FIGURE 5.10

Twin City Manufacturing value stream map, six-month operational review.

belief. Scorecard results showed all seven metrics at 100 percent or better (see Figure 5.11). Cash-to-cash cycle time had improved 230 percent of goal, despite delays in implementation of the supplier inventory replenishment project. Improving cash-to-cash cycle time by 10 days was modest, but had been given a lower priority in their strategic plan as speed, flexibility, and reliability were more important to their goal of regaining market competitiveness. The lesson learned was that working on speed and flexibility to service customers naturally reduced inventories and cash-to-cash cycle time. Fred was particularly happy about this as the bottom line improved by 3 percentage points to 67 percent from 70 percent, and just 3 percentage points short of best in class at 64 percent. The improvement in inventory also freed up 20 percent of their plant's floor space, and while this didn't show up in the current profit and loss, Fred noted it as important to future costs as this space could be used as growth accelerated.

Charlie Dubey reported that he surveyed people from all departments and overall feedback was very positive. The strongest positive came from shop floor team members who expressed only their doubt that to

Twin City Manufacturing SIR Scorecard
Six-Month Operational Review

Key Perspectives	SCOR Level 1 Metrics	Supply-Chain Performance versus Custom Population						☆
		Major Opportunity	Disadvantage	Average or Median	Advantage	Superior	1 yr. Plan
Delivery Performance/ Quality	Delivery performance to request		■		◆	☆ 100%	5%+ 5% $3.9 M/yr
	Perfect order fulfillment		■		◆	☆ 113%	1 yr.1
						100%	+ 31% pts*
Flexibility & Responsiveness	Upside production flexibility	■		☆	△	120%	Required capability
	Order fulfillment lead time (MTO)	■		◆	→ △	150%	−7.5 Days
Cost	Supply-chain management cost	■	☆	◆	→ △	230%	−2.0% $5.2 M/yr
Working Capital	Cash-to-cash cycle time		■	125%	◆	△	10 Day reduction
	Net asset turns		■	☆	◆	→ △	1.2 Turns $19.3 M Inv reduction.
Total Benefit Included in S.C. management cost*		First full year operating profit benefit					$13.0 M
		One time inventory reduction					$19.3 M

■ TCM position   ▽ TCM progress   ◆ Advantage   △ Superior

FIGURE 5.11
Twin City Manufacturing's SIR scorecard, six-month operational review.

management would stick with this plan, but would do what they normally did and change to some new program. Results from other groups were positive, although there was some skepticism. Engineering was concerned that demands for equipment changes would strain their limited resources. Plant maintenance technicians, who had been moved to specific plant areas to be close to the operation they supported, were not sure that this was the best way for them to work.

Production control analysts were initially very skeptical, but with pacemaker scheduling and Kanban systems working plantwide, they felt very good, particularly because for the first time Production Control was actually controlling the plant. Some managers had mixed feedback at this point. They couldn't argue with the results, but this change in thinking—that operators were the only plant people who truly added value directly to the customer—was not yet fully accepted. They were accustomed to past command and control methods and moving to daily shop floor engagement, layered audits and quick response expectations to problems, had reduced their flexibility to do what they wanted to do individually. Top leaders in their group were adapting quickly so this was only a transition issue, but it was clear that 10 percent of current leadership would not succeed in this new Lean System. Charlie recommended that the sooner this was dealt with the better.

Odair had been sitting tapping his foot; finally, he had his chance to present. He had a great story to tell and just wanted to get on with it. He reported on progress with their four top customers and his view of S&OP (Sales and Operations Planning) meetings (Figure 5.12). Odair reported the surveys showed that customers were very pleased with the delivery speed and reliability improvements. In fact, the buyers from LeBlax and Jonso Medical told him that their boss made it clear that if this service improvement continued, he would instruct the sales force to sell TCM products first and substitute another product only when a customer insisted after having been informed about the superior features of TCM products. Buyers from all four companies also indicated they wanted to see more improvement in order processing and other paperwork-related failures as this was still a TCM deficiency. Therefore, this had to be a focus of the project team for the next three months because credibility with key customers must continue to increase.

Odair finished his presentation expressing his satisfaction with the S&OP process, specifically TCM's responsiveness, which allowed Twin

Customer Priorities

TCM Actual Performance	1st Priority	2nd Priority	On-time Delivery	Delivered Quality	Other Delivery Issues	Perfect Order Fulfillment	Order Fulfillment Cycle Time
LeBlax	Delivery reliability	Responsiveness	62%–94.5%	77.4%–90.2%	85%	40.8%–75%	19–9 Days
MexAms	Responsiveness	Delivery reliability	59%–92%	70.3%–83.1%	87%	36.1%–70%	16–7 Days
Jonso Medical	Delivery reliability	Responsiveness	64%–96%	74%–86.8%	84%	39.8%–75%	17–8 Days
Zyxain Medical	Delivery reliability	Responsiveness	60%–96%	79.2%–92%	86%	40.9%–80%	16–8 Days
Overall	Delivery reliability	Responsiveness	61.3%–94.5%	75.2%–88%	85.5%	39.4%–75%	17.0–8.0 Days

Best Performance			On-time Delivery	Delivered Quality	Other Delivery Issues	Perfect Order Fulfillment	Order Fulfillment Cycle Time
LeBlax			88%	88%	99%	85%	9 Days
MexAms			92%	95%	97%	65%	8 Days
Jonso Medical			95%	93%	95%	70%	7 Days
Zyxain Medical			91%	97%	95%	55%	9 Days
Benchmarks			91.5%	93.3%	96.5%	69%	8.25

FIGURE 5.12
Twin City Manufacturing's customer satisfaction survey.

City to take advantage of a competitor's quality and delivery failures by quickly shipping product to help customers not miss their customer delivery dates. He had personally reviewed EVA improvements with their four key customers and they were surprised and pleased by the amount of increased contribution by TCM. Using the EVA analysis with customers had been a grand slam homerun. This teamwork was changing TCM's image from service laggard to service leader. He reported morale in the sales force had never been so high during his twenty-five-year career, and salespeople were having fun making customers happy.

With all the action items from the last meeting completed, Rick made the following points to his team:

1. Great progress has been achieved because we are all working together, pulling the same rope in the same direction.
2. Customers are feeling our improvement as we have established alignment with value in their businesses and we can measure it.

3. We need to spend more shop floor time between review meetings coaching people and seeing the next opportunities.

4. We must protect ourselves against "taking a rest" or complacency, which could set in as our team realizes that we are regaining our number one market position. To do this we must change our thinking about what is possible. Benchmarking has great value, but just being better than the rest at a point in time is not sufficient; we must measure ourselves against perfection, using it as our metric for progress. It is the difference between talking about improving 99 percent quality conformance and reducing the 10,000 parts-per-million defects that exist in our products. We must continually find ways to increase the power of our microscope in order to always have challenging goals that move us closer to perfection. For our next meeting we need to restate our value stream goals in terms of perfection and the gap to achieving it.

Odair interrupted, "But Rick, we have achieved so much and we are in a very strong position. Why do we want to find more ways to make ourselves look bad?" Rick replied, "We must appreciate what we have accomplished. I certainly am very proud of our entire team. We also need to remember that if we don't manage differently, we will likely repeat our past and fall from the number one position again."

Rick and the team then moved to the shop floor where they were each assigned an operation to review. Rick accompanied Eaton Osterlein, as he wanted to coach him on pushing for the next level of improvement. He was confident that a growth surge was imminent and challenged Eaton to push hard for productivity improvement of another 30 percent so that the existing shop floor team members could be used to make the new volume. In addition, the 20 percent available space created from inventory reduction had to be expanded to at least 30 percent of the plant space.

Eaton was thinking as he listened to Rick, "we have already achieved a 15 percent plantwide productivity improvement; where in the world will we find another 30 percent?" They went to the assembly area and started reviewing an audit of automated final assembly completed earlier in the day by the area manager. They talked first with operators about how their jobs were going; they let them know what they were doing there and that they would share the audit summary with them when it was complete.

The standard work instructions are posted at each operation (Figure 5.13). Observing workplace organization and the operator making an order, they found no nonconformance. Rick complimented the operator on her work and asked if she had any suggestions for improving her job. She replied that she had submitted two ideas to her team leader that she thought would allow her to operate three or four machines instead of the current two. Eaton and Rick listened closely as she explained that much of her time is spent checking incoming parts and tooling, loading parts in the machine, and moving finished parts to the pickup area. This is mostly done while the machine sits idle. Output could be increased at least 20 percent just by having the material handler do these tasks. They thanked her for the great suggestions and started to walk back to the conference room. Before Rick could say anything, Eaton blurted out, "OK, I got it; there are huge

Standard Work Instructions		
No. Assembly–03 issue 04	Date: 04-07-05	Name: Dan Friesen
Operation: Automated final assembly order production		
Parts: Metal body, sensors, flexible circuit, connectors		
Tools & Materials: Assembly tooling, conductive adhesive, test fixture		

Step Nbr.	Important Steps	Key Points	Reasons
	A logical segment of the operation when something happens to advance the work in a segment that is transferable	Anything in a step that might— 1. Make or break the job 2. Injure the worker 3. Make the work easier to do, i.e. "knack," "trick," special timing, bit of special information	Reasons for the key points: What defect, safety risk, productivity loss it will prevent
01	Verify and install assembly tooling	1. Engage safety devices at each tooling station	Eliminate risk of injury
		2. Check for and remove excess lubricant	Eliminate quality defects at the customer
		3. When finished check all stations to be sure they are clear of tools and remove safety devices before starting	Eliminate risk of damage to tooling and the equipment
02	Verify parts supplied are correct	Compare parts to the bill of material	Avoid assembling scrap product
03	Clear and fill input material feeders	Make sure all feeders are loaded	Avoid producing assemblies with missing parts
04	Turn on the machine and produce a part	Verify the finished part meets specifications	Eliminates the risk of producing a run of scrap
05	Test the first part	Be sure the part is clamped securely in the test fixture	Eliminate false test readings
06	Remove the part from the test fixture and place in the output container if it passed and in the defects container if it failed		
07	Review failed parts and repeat the start up instructions correcting for the failure cause	If the failure cause is not obvious, stop the operation and turn on the call supervisor light	Problems need to be identified immediately and corrected
08	Place passed parts in the finished product container		
09	Start the machine and run the order		
10	Test the last part made for the order	1. Be sure the part is clamped securely in the test fixture	Eliminate false test readings
		2. If part test good, mark order complete and place the finished parts container on the pick up station	Parts will be picked up by material handler for delivery to packaging

FIGURE 5.13
Standard work instructions.

productivity opportunities in assembly as the value added work content of the operators is extremely low. We have just started to go through each cell again to optimize it with operator balance charts. Maybe your 30 percent improvement is not so ridiculous."

The review team had reassembled and was buzzing about the progress they saw and even more about the many opportunities for improvement shop floor team members and team leaders had told them about. The shop floor teams' enthusiasm had infected them all. Odair had the most telling summary. He told of the operators in packaging (whom he had audited) and their improvements in the past week after visiting with MexAms. They had called the MexAms purchasing agent to get feedback on their last shipment. "It was amazing. I didn't even know there was a problem, and they had already solved it and confirmed it with the customer. Shop floor team members know our key customers personally and respond to their requests without being told. I never would have believed this was possible, but I have seen it with my own eyes."

Eaton then presented five action items for their next review meeting.

1. Charlie and Eaton will see that coaching of the laggards is intensified with the goal of either bringing them up to the needed level or finding a position in the plant where they will be successful in the next three months.
2. Charlie will increase his weekly plant walk-though focusing on auditing safety to get the momentum going in the right direction so results start to improve.
3. A project team will be assigned to improve order processing and other paperwork-related failures during the next three months.
4. The executive team shop floor walk-through will be scheduled a week before next quarter's meeting so results can be summarized and presented at the next meeting.
5. The future-state values stream map will be updated and new targets will be set for improvement, with perfection as the goal.

Rick closed the meeting with an enormous challenge to his team. He told them Eaton had committed to free 30 percent of their plant's floor space and improve productivity another 30 percent. He looked at Odair, and with a wry smile stated, "The ball is in your court. I expect we will all support you in increasing sales 10 percent in the next six months." Odair took it in stride, and thought that with greatly improved operations and leadership from the shop floor team, there was no reason this could not be achieved. He looked at his peers and declared, "You have 100 percent commitment from your sales team; 10 percent growth will be delivered in six months."

Rick went back to his office feeling very satisfied with their progress and couldn't wait to report at next month's quarterly board meeting. He also started to develop plans for how to sustain continuous improvement forever and make it an integral part of TCM's culture. He needed to ensure that all the enabling capability was in place and sustained at levels required for supporting their aggressive goals. Longer term, they had to put in place processes that would continue to push TCM to higher levels of performance even after market leadership was regained.

REFERENCES

Graupp, Patrick, and Robert J. Wrona. *The TWI workbook*. Cambridge, MA: Productivity Press, 2006.

Nakajima, Seiichi. *TPM*. Cambridge, MA: Productivity Press, 1984.

Productivity Development Team. *Just-in-time for operators*. Cambridge, MA: Productivity Press, 1998.

Shingo, Shigeo. *A revolution in manufacturing: The SMED system*. Cambridge, MA: Productivity Press, 1985.

6

The Role of Leadership in Creating a Sustainable Improvement Roadmap

Why is it that two companies, both desiring to make improvements, both with significant opportunity for improvement, with training in the Supply Chain Operations Reference (SCOR) model, Lean, or Six Sigma, and with resources allocated to the task, deliver dramatically different results? Some companies can leverage these three basic requirements into world-class performance while others languish; that is, they talk about improvement but generate minimal real improvement.

The presence of these three core requirements—training, opportunity, and resources—while essential, is not a guarantee of results.

Consider this painful example. A company was quite successful with a record of steady growth and profitability. They were interested in improving their performance because competitive pressures were increasing both domestically and globally. Following a supply chain assessment, numerous and specific improvement opportunities were identified worth approximately 2 percent of revenue. An executive alignment workshop was conducted, basic improvement training was conducted for key staff members, project plans were developed, and a management steering process was put in place. Results? After one year, no significant savings had been booked.

Initial project team meetings were scheduled and conducted with consultants facilitating, but as soon as the consultants stepped aside, the meetings stopped. The forces pushing for change failed to overcome the forces of resistance—therefore no results were achieved. Such stories are tragic because long-term viability of the company is at risk and, along with it, job security and employee well-being.

In previous chapters, methods for creating continuous improvement were explored as we followed Twin City Manufacturing through a cycle of improving its operations. The methodologies are certainly critically important, but not sufficient without underlying support from critical enablers, including

- Culture
- Skills
- Metrics
- Leadership
- Rewards
- Information Systems

CULTURE

The first and most important enabler in this list is culture. What is culture? It is the predominate attitudes and behaviors which characterize the functioning of a group or organization. Culture impacts everything that happens in our organizations from the way customer service representatives behave to the way employees respond to problems. Following are examples of two different cultures. The 3M culture can be described as having the following characteristics:

1. A desire for education and cross-training are valued employee characteristics.
2. The open-door policy is accepted companywide; all employees can approach any management person whenever and wherever they desire.
3. Everyone is on a first-name basis, even the CEO.
4. Chronic complaining isn't welcome; showing initiative is.
5. Mistakes are acceptable as long as they aren't due to negligence or carelessness.
6. Participation at all levels is welcome.
7. Lack of participation is not welcome.

At other companies though, this list might look much different, for example,

1. Mistakes are likely to be fatal. People are fired regularly for unknown reasons.
2. No reward is offered for risk-taking; avoiding blame equals job security.
3. Suggestions are not encouraged.
4. Chain of command is the order of the day.
5. Performance rewards are intermittent and poorly understood.
6. Expediting and firefighting earn the biggest accolades from management.

An important question at this point is: What should a company culture look like in order for it to become an "improvement" company? In a 1985 *Harvard Business Review* article titled "From Control to Commitment," Richard Walton said, "There are two radically different strategies for managing a company's workforce—a strategy based on imposing control and a strategy based on eliciting commitment" (p. 9). Some of the characteristics of these two strategies are listed below:

Control	Commitment
• Individual attention limited to performing individual job	• Individual responsibility extended to upgrading system performance
• Accountability focused on individual	• Frequent use of teams as basic accountable unit
• Fixed job definition conditions	• Flexible definition of duties, contingent on changing
• Measured standards define minimum performance, stability seen as desirable	• Emphasis placed on higher "stretch" objectives," which tend to be dynamic and oriented to the market place
• Structure tends to be layered, with top-down controls	• Flat organization structure with mutual influence systems
• Employees regarded as variable cost	• Assurances that participation will not result in loss of job
• Business information distributed on strictly defined "need to know" basis	• Business data shared widely

Increasing Rate of Improvement

The list on the right suggests a couple of things. First, the level of employee commitment is directly related to the rate of improvement. Traditionally,

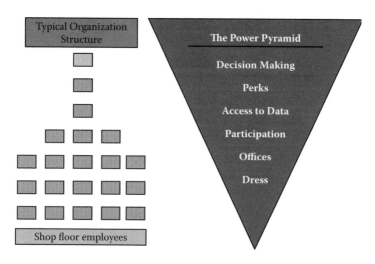

FIGURE 6.1
Typical organization structure.

direct labor employees are viewed as relatively unimportant and as having low decision-making skills. A control-based management process and culture restricts and limits their contributions. If you are serious about continuous improvement, it is important for management to identify this issue and take steps to correct it.

Figure 6.1 is a depiction of a typical organizational structure. It shows that power, including such things as decision making, problem solving, and general business involvement, is often concentrated at the top of the organization even though value added activities are concentrated at the shop floor level. It is a serious fallacy to conclude that only management has anything to contribute. Companies often find that the more their employees behave as co-owners or stakeholders, the better companies perform.

To alter culture, the starting point must be management. It is management's responsibility to outline a vision of their "to-be" culture and style. They must then start by altering their own attitudes and behaviors to support those changes. For example, if employees are expected to exhibit a higher level of ownership and decision making, then some potential changes might include the following:

- Training employees in subjects such as basic problem solving
- Sharing business information
- Asking for employee input and taking it seriously

- Providing opportunities to participate in planning meetings, opportunity identification, and problem-solving teams

LEARNED FROM EXPERIENCE: DAN

EMPLOYEE PROBLEMS MAY BE INDICATIVE OF WORKPLACE PROBLEMS

When I managed a warehouse operation for 3M, I had an employee I would describe as a "problem." This employee seemed unmotivated and was continually being counseled or reprimanded for marginal attendance. Complaints about how things were being done or decisions that were being made were commonplace. I was frustrated and the employee was unhappy.

One day, however, I was surprised to learn that this employee was in charge of the Scout program for the city. He managed a number of scout troops and associated programs and was clearly in charge, making decisions, and ensuring that everything ran smoothly. It was then that I realized the problems at work were with management, that is, with me. I was witnessing firsthand the difference between control performance and commitment performance. The employee was demonstrating far more capability in his personal life than at work. If the workplace functioned differently, he could have taken more of a leading role at work. This is often the case.

Hardly rocket science, but changes such as these require management to reexamine their closely held attitudes and egos.

A second important aspect of company culture is what is recognized and valued by management. If you ask any employee, what it takes to get ahead or achieve recognition at any company, which responses are more likely to be heard—list 1 or 2?

List 1	List 2
Ability to firefight	Teamwork
Whom you know	Initiative
Image/personality	Problem-solving ability
Autocratic style	Ability to communicate

On the flip side, what can get a person fired?

List 1	List 2
Disagreeing with management	Ethics violations
Making a mistake	Negligence
Unpopularity	Poor attendance

Whether done consciously or unconsciously, our companies have a clear reward system that shapes employee behavior. Desired behaviors need to be rewarded. Undesirable behaviors should not be rewarded.

LEARNED FROM EXPERIENCE: DAN

THE CARROT WORKS BETTER THAN THE STICK

At 3M we did not require employees to become cross-trained or volunteer for problem-solving teams, both desired behaviors, but those who did these things received better performance reviews and ultimately more pay and opportunity for advancement.

SKILLS

Skills required for design, management, and improvement of supply chains are required enablers. Skills are sometimes confused with training. Training is essential, but practice and mentoring are also required to build and sustain continuous improvement competencies. Learning basic problem solving is one thing, but it is quite another to execute it by applying this knowledge.

At one company, heavy investments were made in Six Sigma. This included the training of Green Belts, Black Belts, and support staff even including a full-time program director's office to oversee training and project execution. In spite of having all these resources, project after project consumed double the expected time and yielded low or no real savings. Project teams were easily stymied by data collection difficulties, management resistance to change, and the inability to create "perfect" solutions. Although Master Black Belts and champions were in place, they lacked the experience to effectively remove obstacles and set expectations for the teams. Managing significant change for improvement is an experience that few, if any, have. Since it is a wall that hasn't been breached, no one is quite sure how to do it. The result was a costly program yielding minimal results.

Below are a few issues and examples of the skills needed for the successful completion of a project:

1. *Selecting the right tools*: Six Sigma contains over forty tools or analytical methods that must be learned and applied. Selecting those that best fit the problem can be difficult and requires a certain experience level to be done efficiently. Selecting the wrong tools leads to wasted effort and time.

2. *Gather data*: In spite of huge investments in systems, accessing data in the desired format often requires an expert at extracting data and organizing it properly.

LEARNED FROM EXPERIENCE: DAN

ONE THING IS ALMOST CERTAIN: GATHERING DATA WILL BE DIFFICULT

In one company where a supply chain analysis project was undertaken, we determined that on-time delivery data by supply chain was needed. We quickly learned that their systems could not provide this information and we were forced to examine customer orders manually in order to calculate on-time delivery. In another, we needed order history data such as order entry date, ship date, back-order rate, etc. Unfortunately, neither company's IT system could produce the needed data. This sadly is the rule rather than the exception. In the majority of improvement efforts in which I have been involved, the improvement pace was determined by the amount of time required to obtain usable data.

3. *Overcoming obstacles*: A team functions best when someone who has been with the company can innovate when the time comes.

What happens when obstacles arise that stop a project cold? Sometimes a team is ready to implement a solution and management balks. Months of work are wasted when this happens, not to mention the damage to team morale. At one company, the scheduling of production in a large plant had been in the hands of a single individual for years. She was the plant's "go to" person and was on call twenty-four hours a day, seven days a week. A review of her scheduling process revealed that instead of making use of the firm's enterprise resource planning (ERP) system, she employed several forms she had created, a large spreadsheet, and colored pens, which she used to keep track of different products.

In the meantime, their ERP scheduling system was sitting idle. Their system was creating excess inventory of work in progress (WIP) and finished goods, and at times, the right product was not available.

A team was assembled, a project plan was created, and the first two meetings were held. As soon as consultant support was withdrawn, all meetings stopped and the project was dead. "Too busy" was the excuse, but the real reason was that the scheduler, in spite of all the complaints about the job she was doing, did not want to change anything. Management failed to hold the team leader and team accountable for results. Often something as simple as holding people accountable, reworking the business case, or addressing other issues that management perceives as showstoppers is all that is required to keep a project moving forward. It may also require a strong project sponsor to overrule management when their resistance is unjustified.

Metrics

It is imperative that key performance indicators (KPIs) correctly capture and focus our attention on important areas of performance. In Chapter 4, we explored the importance of establishing a *balanced* set of metrics for measuring supply chain performance. This concept of balance ensures that no one performance characteristic is overemphasized. For example, consider the company where the focus of manufacturing was on equipment utilization. Their focus was on running their equipment as much as possible regardless of customer demand or the concept of continuous flow. Consider a company focused on improving delivery performance. In eighteen months they found themselves facing horrendous inventory growth. A company, which focused exclusively on cost, found they lacked the ability to achieve high delivery performance or high responsiveness to customer orders. Lack of balance often leads to unintended consequences. Consider the potential consequences of focusing on a single metric:

Metric	Result When Used Alone
Equipment utilization	Producing more product than needed
On-time delivery	High inventory levels
Unit cost	High inventory levels
Overall cost	Poor service
Production rate	Poor quality

In addition to balance, other characteristics of good metrics can also significantly improve their usefulness. These characteristics are as follows:

1. *Customer alignment—Line of sight to the customer*: Metrics have a way of being created in isolation; that is, they may not have a clear connection to the business, external customers, or shareholders. A well-aligned set of metrics (see Figure 6.2) that reflects customer needs and priorities should be able to survive management changes or any other organizational shifts. Conversely, metrics that reflect the organization more than the customer will always be subject to whim. Unaligned metrics tend to proliferate. It is easy to add metrics but rarely are any eliminated. At a recent client engagement, over 200 metrics were identified within one organization. When analyzed against the "balance" test, some categories were unmeasured and others were grossly overmeasured. A better level and quality of information could have been gathered with less than half the number of the right metrics.

2. *Accuracy:* "Provide a single unvarnished version of the truth." All organizations want their metrics to look good, especially if they are seen as a reflection of performance. This creates an irresistible desire to tweak the numbers. Certain values might not be included because "they are not under our control." In addition, "high flyers" or bad data points may be deleted because there was a "known reason for the problem."

LEARNED FROM EXPERIENCE: DAN

NEVER ASSUME: LOOK FOR HIDDEN PROBLEMS

Recently, we were tracking the origin of a particular on-time delivery metric for a client. In talking with the person responsible for pulling data, we discovered that this individual was responsible for running

(continued)

LEARNED FROM EXPERIENCE: DAN (Continued)

the system query and providing a copy of the data to the department manager, who identified all out-of-spec data points and omitted those that were either explainable or "not under our control."

This approach is typical of a company where organizational concerns are more important than understanding how well the process is working. This has the effect of hiding problems. Leaders must be resolute in encouraging all employees to tell the unvarnished truth. If any flinching or data screening occurs, the ability to identify and solve all the problems that exist is limited. Without honesty, our improvement efforts cannot be properly prioritized.

It takes a concerted effort to let the data tell its story no matter how painful it might be.

3. *Sound metrics:* The metrics must direct effort to the true root causes to ensure results. Once the metric is sound, the next step is to dissect the data in order to understand the root causes of the problems. For example, if order fulfillment cycle time is 10 days, it is necessary to understand how those 10 days break down. (See Figure 6.3) Only then is it is possible to understand where to focus attention so results can be improved.

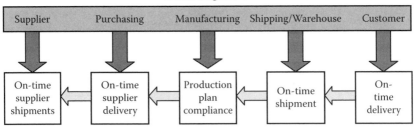

FIGURE 6.2
Metrics alignment.

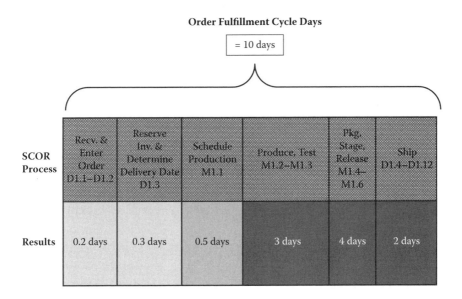

Order Fulfillment Cycle Days

| | = 10 days |

SCOR Process	Recv. & Enter Order D1.1–D1.2	Reserve Inv. & Determine Delivery Date D1.3	Schedule Production M1.1	Produce, Test M1.2–M1.3	Pkg, Stage, Release M1.4–M1.6	Ship D1.4–D1.12
Results	0.2 days	0.3 days	0.5 days	3 days	4 days	2 days

FIGURE 6.3
Order fulfillment cycle.

LEADERSHIP

Making decisions is the role of leadership, who should be focused on the decisions only leaders can make. By encouraging and expecting people at all organizational levels to make decisions that are within their scope of authority, everyone becomes committed to organizational goals and projects. Before making a decision or committing to a specific improvement project goal, leaders must ensure that their executive teams understand the answers to the following questions:

• Where are we as a company?
• Where do we need to be?

Without answers to these two questions, improvement efforts can be aimless and subject to the opinions and whims of everyone in the company who is stakeholder in improvement initiatives.

The question of "where are we" relies heavily on our earlier discussion of accuracy. The question of "where we need to be" is a leadership question. Several strategies can be used to answer this question. The most common ones are the following:

1. *Incremental goal setting:* This means a modest improvement is selected, added to the charts, and then tracked through the year to monitor progress toward the target. Using this method, goals the organization knows it can hit are set. Goal-setting like this keeps stress levels low and applies little pressure to the organization. It fails to sustain a constructive organization tension and ensures the rate of improvement will be slow.

2. *Stretch goal setting:* Stretch goal setting on the other hand increases the pressure and requires some planning to identify *how* the goal will be achieved; it requires rigorous follow up to keep improvement plans on track.

3. *Benchmarking:* As discussed in Chapter 4, benchmarking refers to the level of performance the business requires relative to its competitors or other industry participants. This can be a great way to capture organizational interest and buy-in senior management, but it may not be the most aggressive way to approach improvement.

4. *Perfection:* The idea of perfection is a strategy that stimulates innovation. Perfection means an organization must ask itself the questions: What would order fulfillment cycle time, cost, or on-time delivery be if everything ran perfectly? If there were no waste, rework, errors, etc., what would the order fulfillment cycle time be? Identifying perfection performance levels causes organizations to think about problem solving in a very different way.

The business environment is moving at a rate requiring much more than incremental change to sustain competitiveness. The goal-setting choices leaders make are a test of their leadership ability. Leaders take risks and stretch their organizations to reach beyond what they know can be done. A clear metric with a clear target leads to action and provides a good barometer of success as it allows executive leadership teams to ask themselves "Where are we?" and "Where do we need to go?"

LEARNED FROM EXPERIENCE: DAN

LEADERSHIP MEANS PUSHING THE ORGANIZATION BEYOND ITS LIMITS

While producing diskettes for 3M, we improved unit cost 20 percent per year for more than 10 consecutive years. Our perfection target was still out of reach. We needed to reduce cost another 40 percent. While brainstorming ways to meet our goal, someone asked, "Why do we have to cover both sides of the diskette with fabric? What if we used only enough fabric to clean the recording surface? At first this seemed like a crazy idea, but after testing it, we found it not only was feasible, but also improved other performance characteristics of the product. An incremental goal would never have identified this potential solution.

Organizations should have the fewest KPIs possible to provide a balanced view of performance and unvarnished measures with clear justifiable targets. Much like equipping a car with a dashboard, it should provide enough information to understand how the car is performing and identify desired performance ranges without distracting the driver with too many gauges.

REWARDS

The lack of alignment of metrics and rewards is frequently an obstacle to supply chain performance. Sustainable supply chain competitive advantage is not achievable in organizations with conflicting metrics among various functions. If manufacturing is measured mostly on cost, they are likely to make it a higher priority than service and inventory to meet their objectives. When sales are measured only on top-line sales, they are likely to sell products that are easier to sell regardless of the profit margin or capacity available.

Company leadership must ensure that the metrics and rewards systems of all functions are tightly aligned in support of supply chain performance improvement. SCOR methodology facilitates the alignment and prioritization of metrics across organizations to increase supply chain improvement success probability.

IT SYSTEMS

Effective information systems are fundamental to institutionalizing the processes, practices, data, and metrics that support continuous improvement. Effective continuous improvement activities are data driven and availability of data expressed through supply chain metrics is critical to process analysis and decision making.

The use of SCOR's hierarchical decomposition models (see Chapter 3) allows users to begin at supply chain Level 1, and progress to deeper levels until analysis identifies and ranks improvement opportunities. This generates a true end-to-end view of a company's supply chain.

This view often changes one's perspective about company business data, how it should be defined in databases, and used to measure and operate desired processes and practices. Traditionally, data tends to be readily available along business unit lines and primarily for financial reporting. For example, cost of goods sold (COGS) data is readily available by business unit, but if a business unit consists of three supply chains, measurement and process data will not be available without manual or ad hoc manipulation. The same thing occurs when measuring on-time delivery, order fulfillment cycle time, inventory days of supply, and so on.

The question is, what is required from company systems to bring more value to business processes, effective process measurement, and improvement activities? When it comes to upgrading our IT systems, it is common to put the cart before the horse. To optimize supply chain processes and to support continuous improvement, the following questions should be answered before making a major IT investment.

- Is current data integrity sufficient?
- Do process and systems islands exist because there are multiple sources of data?
- Are there clear owners and governance rules for company data?
- What supply chains are being supported?
- How well are these processes functioning now?
- Should poor processes be streamlined or automated first?

- What processes within these supply chains require IT support that is not currently available?
- Is data defined and organized in databases to support a single source for use in end-to-end processes across the company?
- What information is needed from company systems to effectively measure company supply chains?
- Is company supply chain data organized to provide a product view and market segment/channel view?

An important but little-understood fact is that systems must be configured during installation to provide data and information that enables company business processes. Undertaking a systems implementation or upgrade without answering the above questions will likely lead to disappointment because the new or modified information system doesn't support the way the business is run or the way supply chains are managed.

The processes must be well defined and operated to truly support a company's business models before IT investments are made. Once systems are configured, it is extremely expensive to later decide that the initial configuration doesn't fit the business models, support processes, and specific practices that collectively define a company's competitive difference. Spending a year or more on the front end in order to make sure that current processes are well understood and that a "to be" state with all data requirements is defined is a sound investment for success in any IT system upgrade or new installation.

Another common failure is the temptation to move quickly to IT systems to "help" implement a supply chain or Lean System before having reduced a process to actual practice. Operating a process manually in order to ensure thorough understanding can be invaluable when it comes time to design the IT process. Most people do not understand the processes being performed by the computer. They view it as a black box. Even though manual processes appear inefficient, it is often the best way to confirm the existence of firsthand process knowledge.

Lean, for example, relies heavily on simple, visual, transparent systems. Lean visual management increases everyone's involvement and strengthens the functionality of a team. The Lean operating system is built on the premise that only the direct production operations team member adds value; therefore, IT systems must be designed and implemented in support of the frontline operators.

Another common type of failure that happens to companies installing new IT systems is not defining their processes and ensuring that chosen practices can be properly enabled by the system. Every IT system is standardized by programming logic, which defines how the user is to apply the system. In other words, it defines implied processes or process alternatives the system has the ability to enable. If a company does nothing with their processes prior to implementing a system, the implied processes are *forced* upon the organization, which may not be prepared to completely change the way they work.

IT systems are important to effective supply chain management, but they must be designed to enable the operational processes, not define them. Failure to have clear and well-defined processes that are to be enabled will result in significant disappointment after the IT system's implementation. This failure has led to catastrophic consequences for some companies.

Another issue that frequently causes failure is a company's IT organization structure. It should not stand alone but should have strong connections through the reporting structure to operational groups. This ensures IT does not become an entity unto itself and is not making decisions in a vacuum. Only when IT designs have a supply chain perspective and are built to support the desired end-to-end processes can maximum functionality and value for investments be achieved.

REFERENCE

Walton, Richard. "From Control to Commitment." *Harvard Business Review*. March–April (1985).

7

The Role of Absolute Commitment in Creating and Maintaining Sustainable Improvement

Constancy of purpose—absolute commitment to TPS (Toyota Production System)—is the major factor contributing to Toyota's becoming the world's number one car company. Toyota's leadership actually understands TPS as indicated by the way they manage operations; in addition, every Toyota plant uses the same operating system.

Is it really any wonder that Toyota's service, quality, inventory, and profitability are the industry benchmarks? Their executives believe strategy only becomes real to customers as they experience it through the excellence of their supply chain execution. Customer and market expectations are constantly changing, but Toyota has built their operational system to be adaptive, while at the same time, it is the industry's most efficient. They have a total business model designed and operated every day in every detail to ensure customers experience the Toyota brand promise.

Every company needs to have its version of the Toyota Production System, a system with core principles that do not change over decades and are imbedded in leadership's thinking and the company's culture and rituals. This is an extremely challenging goal for most companies, but one that is a stewardship obligation of CEOs and their executive teams. Currently, most companies are a long way from having their version of TPS, but they must start where they are with purposeful commitment to build this important capability to ensure current and future company success.

Frequently, supply chains evolved over years rather than being purposefully designed, resulting from organizations having not given much thought to supply chain design as a significant factor in performance. It is still not the norm for companies to place thoughtful emphasis on improving total supply chain performance to gain competitive advantage. Supply chain benchmarking, target setting, and improvement planning should be a standard part of every business's strategic plan and planning process. The planning process should answer several important questions:

- Which performance metrics should be used?
- Which ones are most related to business success?
- What capability is most important to improve?

These critical questions deserve thoughtful analysis before responses are defined. In most companies, operations has the greatest resources to support improvement projects. These precious resources should be focused very precisely on the most important improvement needed. However, it is common for targets to be arbitrary and unrelated to differentiated performance that customers will pay for in price or with a larger share of a product category.

Multimarket companies frequently set supply chain performance goals companywide, a practice that can only be described as value destroying. Investments in supply chain benchmarking research are as valuable as in market research. Identifying market growth opportunities will only turn into sales and profits if operational execution levels are sufficient to enter and win business, especially if the business must be taken from a competitor. Supply chain assessment, target setting, and implementation planning must be an important component of business strategic planning for any company serious about achieving sustainable operational excellence.

Some companies, who are suppliers to such industries as automotive or consumer retail, have been forced to develop a level of excellence to meet their customers' expectations; others commonly focus on some specific performance metric that is viewed as a disadvantage or simply because cost of goods sold is the largest expense for most companies.

Assuming a company has a strong strategic supply chain plan, skills and knowledge are required to turn plan capability and performance requirements into reality. Supply chain expertise is seldom viewed as a strategic capability that must be built and sustained, supplying needed leadership and support for supply chain improvement initiatives. Supply chains are not thought of as areas for investment in highly skilled people in the same way most companies invest in product, technology, and marketing, yet it is operational excellence or the lack of it that customers feel. Supply chain excellence is about strategy. Unfortunately, operational excellence is often pigeonholed into being about cost or a reaction to a loss of business or top position with a key customer. Significant investment choices are often made by considering only factory cost benefits, or at best their total delivered cost, without understanding the effect on inventory, service, responsiveness, and flexibility of the supply chain.

Today, with rapidly increasing transportation costs and exploding growth in developing markets, companies are forced to rethink supply chains to compete in global markets. Many companies have missed opportunities for lack of forward thinking, investments in supply chain modeling, research, and highly skilled professionals. Supply chain knowledge professionals can model supply chains that enable companies to continually develop improvement options, stay abreast of best practices and sustain regular benchmarking versus peer companies in their markets.

There are five practices that every company should invest in to drive better decision making and continually improve supply chain performance's contribution to competitive advantage. They should be a part of the strategic and operational planning of every company. They are as follows:

1. Proper design of supply chains
2. SCOR customer satisfaction performance benchmarking
3. Financial performance benchmarking
4. SCOR process benchmarking
5. Assessment versus supply chain maturity models.

LEARNED FROM EXPERIENCE: PAUL

SOUND MODELING IS ESSENTIAL TO SUPPORT INVESTMENT DECISION MAKING

At the end of 2003, I became corporate vice president of 3M Supply Chain Services. Among our responsibilities was supporting the wide range of 3M businesses in order to improve their supply chains.

(continued)

LEARNED FROM EXPERIENCE: PAUL (Continued)

At the time, there were no people left who focused on supply chain modeling to support businesses in making better design choices.

3M has among the best total global reach of any company in the world, particularly for its size. Manufacturing in more than sixty countries, utilizing an extremely broad range of technologies, and producing products shared across many markets are great strengths of 3M, but it is also a complicated environment in which to make choices about investing in new capability and requires sound modeling to support investment decision making.

We made three investments to move 3M capability forward: We hired highly skilled professionals, purchased modeling software, and developed a rigorous methodology for making supply chain investment choices. These capabilities were quickly in high demand by our internal clients because of their meaningful contribution to 3M businesses.

HOW TO PROPERLY DESIGN SUPPLY CHAINS

Most supply chains are products of evolution. Their current state results from many changes often made over an extended period. Everything in all supply chains is constantly changing—suppliers and supplier performance, customers and their expectations, product designs, production processes, business rules, etc.

Change constantly makes its way into supply chains and, for several reasons, frequently goes unrecognized. First, unless a robust supply chain dashboard is in place, small changes in performance can go unnoticed. Second, very few people have their eye on the entire supply chain. People live and work in their own functional corner of the business. Until they reach the highest organizational levels, few people are aware of end-to-end performance or, if they are, they find it difficult to convince others to change. Even the idea of "designing" a supply chain is rare in most companies.

LEARNED FROM EXPERIENCE: DAN

IN LAUNCHING A NEW PRODUCT, THE TENDENCY IS TO IMPLEMENT A FLOW MUCH LIKE ONE USED BEFORE; THIS CAN BE AN ERROR

While working with a client recently, I was asked to help design a supply chain for a new product that was to be launched in two years. As we began to identify customers, suppliers, and so on, I asked if a path had been identified for the flow of materials, work, and information. The answer was "Yes!" In the absence of a new design, they were moving to implement a flow much like an older existing product. Upon completing a flow map of existing products, the client quickly identified design changes to make. This is our tendency.

If current models are working, the tendency is to gravitate toward staying with them unless someone intervenes or a crisis occurs. Unfortunately, this approach ensures that new supply chains will follow the pattern of current designs with all of their problems, issues, and shortcomings. It takes vision and courage to rethink and replace existing systems and processes. Supply chain design must consider these factors:

- Customers and markets served
- Customer and market supply chain expectations
- The development of a meaningful supply chain dashboard
- Material flow design
- Work and information flow design
- Level 1 metrics (SCOR Level 1) aligned upstream to suppliers and suppliers' suppliers if possible
- Financial effect
- Project management capability
- Operational capabilities
- Risk management
- Alignment with business strategies

HOW TO DEFINE CUSTOMERS AND THEIR EXPECTATIONS

As demonstrated in Chapter 4, a clear understanding of who your customers are and what must be done to successfully compete for and win their business is essential. For most businesses, customers can be segmented into multiple groups, each with its own unique needs and expectations. For example, mass merchandisers such as Wal-Mart and Target have very different supplier expectations than OEMs (original equipment manufacturers), distributors, government customers, or others have of theirs.

Supply chain designs that meet low cost expectations may not look the same as those designed for maximum responsiveness. This is the power of the SCOR methodology and its decomposition model. Starting with the service metrics, which reflect the most important attributes of any customer, SCOR links multilevel metrics to Level 1 process definitions, which must be designed using current best practices or by innovating new ones in order to ensure that the capability exists to achieve targeted levels of performance of selected top-level metrics.

HOW TO CREATE A SUPPLY CHAIN DASHBOARD

Few design activities will be as important as selecting Level 1 metrics that will provide needed visibility into how the supply chain is performing. Doing this correctly dictates leaving aside organizational and individual paradigms, current metrics, and opinions. The goal is to create a dashboard that provides the following:

1. Balanced view of performance with both external (customer)-facing and internal-facing metrics
2. Organization that measures performance along supply chain lines
3. Unflinching measurements; that is, metrics designed to reveal actual performance
4. Links to actions; that is, metrics that reveal actual performance compared with required performance
5. Performance targets aligned with business objectives

HOW TO DESIGN MATERIAL FLOW

1. Once competitive priorities are understood, a "to be" material flow plan should be developed incorporating desired best practices and addressing disconnects in the material flow of existing products. Key questions to ask before designing a material flow plan include the following:

   - Who are the key suppliers and where are they located?
   - What internal company locations will be part of the supply chain?
   - What is the distance to (key) markets and what is the transit time to customers? This is a leading indicator of service and inventory levels.
   - What is the distance from (key) suppliers and what is the transit time from suppliers to the company's plant locations? This is a leading indicator for inventory and supply reliability.
   - What is the overall supply chain cycle time?
   - What are the operational capabilities of the supply chain?
   - What is the organizational rating of the quality and availability of a workforce capable of operating and improving production?
   - What specific functional expertise is required and is it available to supply chain locations?
   - What is the supplier rating of local practices for managing suppliers?
   - What about the design?
   - How will the product be distributed and what distribution facilities are involved?
   - Which disconnects within existing material flows should be eliminated?
   - What material flow is required to achieve targeted supply chain performance?

Network design options developed should be modeled using one of the many available software modeling tools. These tools allow users to enter all known factors related to unit labor cost, local materials cost, transportation, duties, and many more to allow modeling of outcomes for each scenario related to service predictability, cost, inventory levels, total transportation costs, etc.

Tools such as SCOR supply chain mapping identify high-level supply chain structures or scenarios of various structures. Details about these scenarios can then be developed to load modeling tools with complete data to determine how a proposed supply chain will perform.

Supply chain models can also be used to evaluate and assess risk, such as increases in transportation costs. What if labor cost inflation increases? What if the government increases or decreases import taxes? Design scenarios can be challenged by a multifunctional team to be sure assumptions and risk assessments are as valid as possible. Modeling tools and highly skilled professionals trained to use them are critical to making smart decisions.

HOW TO DESIGN WORK AND INFORMATION FLOW

In an approach similar to designing material flow, key transactional processes such as order management, purchasing, work orders, and planning cycles should be examined for improvement opportunities. Process mapping of current processes can identify practices that need to be improved.

SCOR's decomposition structure provides a structure to ensure all necessary elements of each needed process are considered during mapping. SCOR's "as is" mapping process creates detailed step-by-step documentation of how information and documents flow through a company. This gives the opportunity to see and identify disconnects and defects throughout the process. Identified disconnects and defects can then be resolved using problem-solving tools that result in process improvement.

The last step is to create a "to be" process map. This SCOR map can be used to show the process once all disconnects and defects are resolved, or it can be used to define a new process that might streamline the flow. Usually these more radical change proposals require upgraded or new information technology tools to enable proposed processes and practices.

RISK CONSIDERATIONS

Projects always include myriad assumptions about such issues as resources, timelines, import and export laws and regulations, intellectual property protection, expected changes in transportation, duties, and handling costs. All project assumptions have associated risks that affect the probability of achieving each assumption. The risks related to each assumption must be assessed to determine if they have a significant probability of happening or a low probability of happening but with a catastrophic effect on the project. Once these critical risks are identified, plans must be developed to mitigate their consequences should they occur.

- What is the project's timeline?
- Are the required resources identified and available to complete the project on time?
- What human resource and spending uncertainties exist?
- What happens if supply chain cost factors increase?
- What operating costs or performance risks exist that will result if expected values are not met?
- What risk exists with new supply chains that could adversely affect performance resulting in a loss of revenues?
- What intellectual property–related risks exist?

FINANCIAL CONSIDERATIONS

The direct or indirect goal of improvement projects is improving financial performance. It is critical to understand specifically how projects will affect the final financial results. These questions and the customer and supplier economic value added tool shown in Figure 4.3. allow you to evaluate projects based on the effect they will have on financial results.

- What net impact on operating income will result from changes to factory cost, freight, duties, and other costs?
- What are the potential tax consequences of each alternative?
- What will effective income tax rates do to changes in operating income?
- What will be the working capital effect of design alternatives?

HOW TO MEASURE CUSTOMER SATISFACTION

Lean, Six Sigma, and SCOR all agree that the customer is king. No business exists without customers, so it is fundamental to have a way to measure customer satisfaction. Measurements must align with customer needs and expectations, be measurable, and simple enough to be easily understood by all employees. SCOR lists three customer-facing performance attributes:

- Delivery reliability
- Responsiveness
- Flexibility

The Supply Chain Council recommends a supply chain scorecard (Level 1) contain at least one metric from each of these categories. These are subsequently decomposed to lower-level metrics. For example, perfect order fulfillment is a common Level 1 metric under the delivery reliability attribute. Perfect order fulfillment is typically composed of percent of orders delivered on time, percent of orders delivered with no damage, percent of orders delivered in full, and percent of orders delivered with correct paperwork. Though not listed in the SCOR model, percent of orders delivered meeting customer specifications is often added as well. These Level 1 and 2 metrics meet the criteria mentioned in the first paragraph in this section.

HOW TO CREATE A MATURITY MODEL

Many supply chain consulting companies have developed maturity models. One example comes from PRTM Consulting—the Supply Chain Maturity Model created in 2000; it is described in *Strategic Supply Chain Management* (2005). PRTM's Maturity Model describes four stages: Stage one is functional focus, stage two is integration, stage three is external integration, and stage four is cross-enterprise collaboration.

PRTM's research demonstrated strong correlation between performance and the maturity stage of a particular practice. If, for example, a company's planning practices are assessed as practices associated with maturity stage three, it is highly probable that supply chain performance related to planning will also exhibit a performance level commensurate with stage three practice. The power of this model is in measuring the current practice level using a scale that represents best practices regardless of industry. This is something that should be used at some frequency—every two or three years—to calibrate the business's current practice state versus state of the art.

Companies who are in the top tier of supply chain performers in their market will also find this model useful as their maturity model because it is particularly powerful for generating new levels of capability that will help them maintain their leadership position.

Edward Deming talked repeatedly throughout his career about constancy of purpose. This is a hard principle to imbed in a company over time with changing executives and market pressures for quarterly performance. It is also one of the most important for companies if they are to be able to survive and maintain excellence through decades. A critical factor in achieving constancy of purpose is building supply chain strategic planning into company rituals in a way that is market relevant.

No competent CEO is going to come into a company and, in the annual planning rituals, modify practices that obviously demonstrate the addition of value for customers. This is particularly true if other executive team members are strong supporters of this practice. Strategic supply chain planning must be owned by every company's executive committee; it must be understood and practiced as a key responsibility of company leadership.

CHALLENGES TO MAINTAINING YOUR COMPANY'S SUPPLY CHAIN

Too often business leaders underestimate the scope and difficulty in designing, implementing, managing, and improving supply chains. It has become increasingly hard in the last two decades of globalization and constant change in political and trade conditions, emerging markets, and global information. Competitive advantage is short lived as companies from any country can reach markets anywhere. Conduct an Internet search for almost any product, and you will find global sources that are ready and willing to sell and deliver products.

This means investment mistakes quickly become a disadvantage. Making an incremental investment in home country capacity seems cheaper than building a new site in emerging markets and from a short-term cost standpoint is often cheaper. However, not having a strong supply chain in place to support growing a local business in an emerging market will have serious and damaging consequences that can take years to rectify. These are very difficult decisions with significant financial consequences requiring thorough analysis, plans to manage risk, and a longer horizon than a decision based on immediate considerations.

For a supply chain to be successful, every company needs to adopt a rigorous methodology as a key component of maintaining supply chain excellence.

LEARNED FROM EXPERIENCE: PAUL

ADAPT TO LOCAL BEHAVIORS AND BUILD A CORE SUPPLY CHAIN OR SUFFER THE CONSEQUENCES

While I was managing director of 3M Brazil, one of the biggest U.S. retailers entered the Brazilian market. It did not go well. It had some strong regional competitors, including French retailer Carrefour, which started much earlier and was entrenched in key cities across Brazil.

In addition, the U.S. retailer, which had built its competitive advantage on supply chain superiority, made a series of significant mistakes that ranged from not understanding local market behaviors to not building a strong local supply chain to support its first stores. For example, after many years of high inflation, Brazilians were accustomed to buying their monthly necessities as soon as they received their paychecks. In addition, local retailers and Carrefour built their stores with two or more times as many checkout stations than seen in a typical U.S. store.

I went with our local account manager to the opening of the first store. When we arrived, I was shocked to see that the large parking lot was half-full of tents; material was piled everywhere; it was an incredible mess. I knew that my sales manager had been called by the store's commodity buyers many times to assist them in finding some 3M products located in the tents.

(continued)

LEARNED FROM EXPERIENCE: PAUL (Continued)

When we entered the store, we saw customers waiting to check out in a line that ran all the way to the back wall of the store. Before we finished our visit, we noticed people walking out and leaving their carts. The consequences of this failure to adapt to local behaviors and build a core supply chain were serious and set back their expansion plans by years.

THE IMPORTANCE OF TRAINING

One irrefutable fact is that leadership in any endeavor is a first-order requirement. Yet far too often it is thought this will happen automatically, that employees will learn and gain experience from the managers they work with and the school of hard knocks. This is unrealistic. Most people's early career years involve working in limited positions and frequently in one functional area of their company. This is not sufficient, as people must develop a working knowledge of all enterprise functions, which only happens if there is a purposeful development program in place. In addition, working on cross-functional teams as well as learning to lead and follow are all necessary skills. They must also learn to overcome difficult challenges, achieve challenging goals, and demonstrate the ability to lead an organization to be its best. It can no longer be acceptable to allow leadership development to just happen; companies cannot afford the cost of failure that results from this approach.

LEARNED FROM EXPERIENCE: PAUL

DEVELOPING LEADERSHIP IS ESSENTIAL TO A COMPANY'S SUCCESS

During four years of Jim McNerney's leadership at 3M, he personally led Six Sigma implementation, which he repeatedly said was principally a leadership development program. This was reality as Black Belts and Master Black Belts faced very challenging targets in cost, growth, and working capital improvement.

(continued)

LEARNED FROM EXPERIENCE: PAUL (Continued)

Because they also worked on projects across all company functions, this project depth gave them a meaningful learning experience about other functions. In addition, a leadership development program and multimillion-dollar facility to house this program was high on McNerney's agenda. Great leadership was reinforced as his highest priority to improve 3M performance.

SET STRETCH GOALS

There is always an argument between the "go-for-it guys" and the incrementalists who believe in setting realistic and achievable goals. The trouble with incremental goals is that, too often, current thinking and practices are enough to achieve these incremental goals, but if significant improvement is needed, stretch goals, sometimes even ridiculous goals, are essential.

Stretch goals, which people realize can't possibly be achieved with their current thinking and practices, force people to examine all current assumptions and search for other ideas and perspectives. Stretch goals challenge an organization to reach levels they did not think were possible and, when properly managed, are very motivating.

LEARNED FROM EXPERIENCE: PAUL

BUILD STRETCH GOALS INTO YOUR ORGANIZATION'S OPERATING PLAN

During my plant manager years, we adopted stretch goals to improve the cost of diskettes. We repeatedly set targets that we had no idea how to achieve. After some success, this process became almost an addiction for the organization, which had experienced a high from achieving what appeared to be impossible goals.

(continued)

LEARNED FROM EXPERIENCE: PAUL (Continued)

Later, this experience was reinforced under Jim McNerney's leadership at 3M. Six Sigma goals for every organization worldwide were very challenging and most people had never experienced making improvement at the rate required to achieve these goals. With experience and success, confidence grew and a general excitement and pride accompanied the success of 3M organizations. Once established, some percentage of expected improvement was built into every organization's operating plan.

Every business must have a road map that provides direction to its organization and creates a compelling case for change. We only have to examine Toyota to know that a roadmap and compelling case must be implemented to achieve excellence in operational processes. The road map always has the same destination—satisfying existing customers and creating new satisfied customers.

There have to be a strategy and tactical plans that include and align marketing, product development, and supply chain. Frequently, companies rely on their personal knowledge of customers and markets in addition to market research to bring in outside information, improving the quality of their plan. They are also very comfortable investing in product development to maintain the value of their current offering or to introduce truly new products to the world.

Supply chain is a different matter. A lot of money is spent on plants and distribution centers, but little is normally invested in process and people capability, the factors that are most critical to supply chain contribution. How many strategic plans actually describe the specific capability required from company supply chains? How many strategic plans use outside research to quantify best market performance in delivery, flexibility, and responsiveness?

Strategic plans without a supply chain component are really a statement of intentions, as the operational capability to source, plan, make, deliver, and manage returns to meet the strategic plan requirements is simply assumed. Top business leaders can no longer afford to assume supply chains will perform to meet their business plan; they must include a supply chain component in all strategic business plans.

IMPLEMENT AN EVALUATION PROCESS

Each decision adds a brick to today's path or builds a new path. All supply chain investment, whether it is skilled people, facilities, equipment, or IT systems, must be very carefully evaluated. The evaluation process, in addition to validating alignment to strategic objectives, must look at end-to-end outcomes of service, costs, and working capital. It must examine operational capability to be certain it will be sufficient.

Too frequently an overly simplified cost evaluation becomes the decision driver. The evaluation process must include consideration of a wide range of factors that contribute to end performance and simulations to test assumptions and risk. It is important to think about the direction in which a specific investment decision is taking the business. Is it building another brick on the present path or is it creating a new path, one that is linked to future growth and management of risk? We need to be sure to seek the best, not just the good.

COMMIT YOURSELF TO HANDS-ON LEADERSHIP—DON'T DELEGATE

Business success is built and sustained customer by customer. The only reality of a supplier's brand promise is their customer's everyday product and service experience. Customers experience a company's supply chain through every transaction and touch point. Without supply chain excellence, brand promises are empty promises. Sustainable market leading businesses use their supply chain as a competitive weapon to protect existing business, respond to opportunities more effectively than competitors, and increase customer share by taking business from competitors. There are no examples of long-term sustainable market leading companies that don't have supply chains that effectively deliver their competitive advantage to customers every day.

There are five final thoughts for business leaders to take and apply to their company's supply chain.

1. Supply chain is too important to business success to leave it solely in the hands of company manufacturing executives. This is not to say business leaders must be supply chain experts—they don't, but it is important to have a sufficient working knowledge to be able to integrate into strategic and operational planning, set necessary performance targets, and assess supply chain performance.
2. Invest in educating top leadership team members in supply chain improvement methodologies and making a collective commitment to implementation. Have them all read this book as a starting point to gain a working knowledge is only a matter of investing some time in learning the essence and fundamentals of SCOR, Lean, and Six Sigma. This investment will have a significant and lasting return.
3. Develop the three-to-five-year supply chain vision required to support the growth, income and return goals. Use the Sustainable Lean Improvement Roadmap as a winning plan model.
4. Invest in companywide leadership of the supply chain excellence initiative that is positioned and resourced for success.
5. Hold all leadership team members accountable for active leadership and participation in making implementation of your company's Sustainable Lean Improvement Roadmap successful.

It is time to fix your supply chain!

REFERENCE

Cohen, Shoshanah, and Joseph Rousel. *Strategic supply chain management.* New York: McGraw Hill, 2005.

Resources

TRAINING SERVICES

Sigma Breakthrough Technologies—Six Sigma Training
Lean Enterprise Institute—Lean training courses
Supply Chain Council—SCOR training

BOOKS

Valuable Books about Lean

Andy and Me, Pascal Dennis, Cambridge, MA: Productivity Press, 2005.

The Toyota Way, Jeffrey Liker, New York: McGraw-Hill, 2004.

The Machine That Changed the World, James Womack, Daniel Jones, and Daniel Roos, New York: Rawson Associates, 1990.

TPM Introduction, Seiichi Nakajima, Cambridge, MA: Productivity Press, 1988.

Lean Thinking, James Womack and Daniel Jones, New York: Free Press, 2003.

The SMED System, Shigeo Shingo, Cambridge, MA: Productivity Press, 1985.

Lean Production Simplified, Pascal Dennis, Cambridge, MA: Productivity Press, 2002.

Zero Quality Control, Shigeo Shingo, Cambridge, MA: Productivity Press, 1986.

Toyota Production System, Taiichi Ohno, Cambridge, MA: Productivity Press, 1988.

The New Manufacturing Challenge, Kiyoshi Suzaki, New York: Free Press, 1987.

Implementation Tools

The Toyota Way Fieldbook, Jeffery Liker and David Meier, New York: McGraw-Hill, 2006.

Creating a Lean Culture, David Mann, Cambridge, MA: Productivity Press, 2005.

Mistake-Proofing, Cambridge, MA: Productivity Press, 1987.

Quick Changeover, Cambridge, MA: Productivity Press, 1986.

Just-in-Time for Operators, Cambridge, MA: Productivity Press, 1988.

TPM for Every Operator, Cambridge, MA: Productivity Press, 1996.

Kanban for the Shopfloor, Cambridge, MA: Productivity Press, 2002.

Getting the Right Things Done, Cambridge, MA: Lean Enterprise Institute, 2006.

Learning to See, Mike Rother and John Shook, Cambridge, MA: Lean Enterprise Institute, 2003.

Creating Level Pull, Art Smalley, Cambridge, MA: Lean Enterprise Institute, 2004.

Creating Continuous Flow, Mike Rother and Rick Harris, Cambridge, MA: Lean Enterprise Institute, 2001.

Making Materials Flow, Rick Harris, Chris Harris, and Earl Wilson, Cambridge, MA: Lean Enterprise Institute, 2003.

The TWI Workbook, Patrick Graupp and Robert Wrona, Cambridge, MA: Productivity Press, 2006.

Reference Books

The Encyclopedia of Operations Management, Art Hill, Cambridge, MA: Clamshell Beach Press, 2007.

Lean Lexicon, Cambridge, MA: Lean Enterprise Institute, 2006.

REFERENCES

Chapter 1

Goldratt, Eli, and Jeff Cox. *The goal*. Great Barrington, MA: North River Press, 1984.

Porter, Michael. *Competitive strategy*. New York: Free Press, 1980.

Treacy, Michael, and Fred Wiersema. *The discipline of market leaders.* Reading, MA: Addison Wesley, 1995.

Womack, James, and Daniel Jones. *Lean thinking.* New York: Free Press, 2000.

Womack, James P., Daniel T. Jones, and Daniel Roos. *The machine that changed the world.* New York: Rawson Associates, 1989.

Chapter 2

Bolsdorf, Peter, and Robert Rosenbaum. *Supply chain excellence.* New York: Amacom, 2003.

Goldratt, Eli, and Jeff Cox. *The goal.* Great Barrington, MA: North River Press, 1984.

Ohno, Taiichi. *Toyota production system: Beyond large-scale production.* Cambridge, MA: Productivity Press, 1988.

Rother, Mike, and John Shook. *Learning to see.* Cambridge, MA: Lean Enterprise Institute, 2003.

Schonberger, Richard. *Japanese manufacturing techniques.* New York: Free Press, 1982.

Womack, James P., Daniel T. Jones, and Daniel Roos. *The machine that changed the world.* New York: Rawson Associates, 1990.

Chapter 3

Cohen, Shoshanah, and Joseph Roussel. *Strategic supply chain management.* New York: McGraw Hill, 2005.

Lambert, Doug. *Supply chain management.* Sarasota, Florida. Supply Management Institute, 2004.

Lambert, Doug. *Supply chain management.* Sarasota, FL: Supply Management Institute, 2006.

Ohno, Taiichi. *Toyota production system: Beyond large-scale production.* Cambridge MA: Productivity Press, 1988.

Womack, James P., Daniel T. Jones, and Daniel Roos. *The machine that changed the world.* New York: Rawson Associates, 1990.

Chapter 4

Bossidy, Larry. *Confronting reality.* New York: Crown Press, 2004.

Graupp, Patrick, and Robert J. Wrona. *The TWI workbook*. New York: Productivity Press, 2006.

Porter, Michael. *Value chain*, New York: Free Press, 1985.

Porter, Michael. "What is Strategy?" *Harvard Business Review* 74, 6 (1996): 61–78.

Shook, John, and Mike Rother. *Learning to see: Value stream mapping to add value and eliminate MUDA*. Cambridge, MA: Lean Enterprise Institute, 1999.

Treacy, Michael, and Fred Wiersema. *The discipline of market leaders*. Reading, MA: Addison Wesley, 1995.

Chapter 5

Graupp, Patrick, and Robert J. Wrona. *The TWI workbook*. Cambridge, MA: Productivity Press, 2006.

Nakajima, Seiichi. *TPM*. Cambridge, MA: Productivity Press, 1984.

Productivity Development Team. *Just-in-time for operators*. Cambridge, MA: Productivity Press, 1998.

Shingo, Shigeo. *A revolution in manufacturing: The SMED system*. Cambridge, MA: Productivity Press, 1985.

Chapter 6

Walton, Richard. "From Control to Commitment." *Harvard Business Review*. March–April, 1985.

Chapter 7

Cohen, Shoshanah, and Joseph Rousel. *Strategic supply chain management*. New York: McGraw Hill, 2005.

About the Authors

Paul C. Husby completed a 38-year career with 3M that included executive management positions such as managing director of 3M Brazil, vice president of the Abrasives Division, and corporate staff vice president of Manufacturing and Supply Chain Services. He graduated from the University of Wisconsin, Stout, with a BS degree in industrial technology. Paul's career included a significant number of operational leadership assignments in manufacturing, engineering, and supply chain prior to the executive leadership assignments. Twelve years of his career were spent on international assignments in places such as Belgium, the United Kingdom, and Brazil; he speaks Portuguese as a second language. Currently a supply chain consultant with a passion for Lean manufacturing, he is also involved with Hope Unlimited of Brazil as a member of the International Advisory Board. Hope is a nonprofit organization that rescues and transforms the lives of Brazilian street children.

Dan Swartwood is director of Process and Supply Chain Design for Satellite Logistics Group, headquartered in Houston, Texas. Prior to his current position, Dan worked as the director of the Value Chain Center of Excellence for PRAGMATEK Consulting Group. In this role he assisted clients in the aerospace and defense, pharmaceutical, medical, industrial, automotive, chemical, and high-tech industries to analyze their supply chains and identify competitive performance gaps and improvement opportunities. During the first 25 years of his career, he held a wide range of management positions for 3M Company and Imation Enterprises, developing his Six Sigma and Lean skills. He is a Certified SCOR instructor with the Supply Chain Council, a certified CPIM (Certified in Production and Inventory Management) through APICS (the Association for Operations Management), and an American Society for Quality (ASQ) -certified Quality Engineer. Dan frequently speaks on topics in business and business improvement and has published numerous articles. In the area of supply chain technology, Dan has filled many roles within the Supply Chain Council, including member of the board of directors, chairman of the Technical Development Steering Committee, membership in the International Society of Six Sigma Professionals, and Dean's Advisory Council of Arizona State University, West. Dan and his wife Kathy reside in Houston, Texas.

Index